Go Team You!
Encouraging words to support you in the race to becoming the
you I know you can be!
Wise Wei

Go Team Me!!

Without my team's support, I would have fumbled the ball and lost the game!

To my coaches: Dr. and Mrs. Frank E. Brown, my parents, who taught me to believe in me and that every day is a day worth cheering about!

To my cheerleaders who motivated me and kept me going even when my hands cramped and my eyes blurred: Janice Lanier, Yolanda Meaders, Tonya Grant, Natasha Acheampong, Sharon Claggett, Lisa Bolds, Pia Cortes, Solange Perry, Melodee Mifflin, James Davis, Brandon King, Jodi Erickson, Anne Almond, Golder Washington, Keith Harris, Sonja Eley, Kim Hodge, Vanessa Young Russell, Estela Chavarria, Shavon Beans, Karen Cespedes and Sean Washington

To my recruiters, who started me on this route to success: Catherine Bridgett, Yolanda Starke, Kenneth Whaley and Allan Wiggins

To my fabulous photographer: Michael James

To all of my children: William, Maria, Zachary, Daniel, Claudia, Chris and Nicky

To my agent who doubles as my brother for making my dream a reality: Bert Brown and

To God...

HOORAY!! WHO?! RAY (that's me)!

Go Team You!

MISERABLE MONDAY, TIRESOME TUESDAY, "WHAT IT"S ONLY WEDNESDAY?" Wednesday?? Are you living for "TGIF"? If you are do you realize how you are altering your life? Your life span on earth is FINITE, therefore of the 7 days you have been given per week, you have decided that only 3 of them are worth looking forward to which means you are only somewhat content for about 12 days a month. And even that's not accurate if you consider that some time on Sunday afternoon you start thinking about and dreading Monday!!! You are shortening your LIFE!!! Find enjoyment in EVERY FRAGILE, PRECIOUS, EXTRAORDINARY DAY THAT GOD BLESSES YOU WITH, PLEASE. Go Team You!

Food for thought: Everyday without fail we brush our teeth (at least I hope we do). Why? To remove all the "yuck' that has built up within us and after brushing we feel refreshed and renewed. Now how is that different from prayer? Pray daily…Go Team You!

Are you afraid of flying? Is it the fear of not reaching your destination? Do you realize that you have already been cleared for takeoff? You may experience some turbulence along the way but there are no delays and you have not been grounded. In the cockpit is your Captain, willing and able to get you to where you need to be but you must get on board and put your faith in Him. It is time to depart from the norm. So, fasten your safety belt, stow away all excess baggage that may get in your way and prepare to soar!! Go Team You!

Can you read minds? Well neither can I, so why do we waste sooooo much time trying to do exactly that? We try to read someone's actions and or words. "Why did he do that?" "What did she mean when she said that?" We speculate, we ask anyone within earshot to explain to us what happened but what we don't do many times is go to the source and simply ask them, the why or the what. Make the decision to not spend your life worrying and speculating. Mind reading is not your expertise. We must either go to the source or decide to give it to God and move on. Time is way too precious to waste. Go Team You!

Ponder this thought for a moment...why do we cling to, repeat, hover around, refuse to let go, sit in, around, under and on top of things, people and/or behaviors that are, simply put, BAD for us? It's as if the Devil drops by for a visit and instead of making up the guestroom we give him the master suite!! Well, I challenge you today to delete the bad behavior, vices and/or people that have taken up residence in your life. Delete and deliver yourself from the bondage that keeps you from the happiness that you DESERVE! Go Team You!

Tell me your secrets and I'll tell you mine. Sometimes our secret wishes and desires are buried deep in the treasure trove of our psyche because they seem silly and/or we don't believe they will ever come to pass. Well the moment has come to speak them into the atmosphere and make your secrets a reality. What do you have to lose and more importantly how much could you gain? Don't allow your desires and wishes to remain a secret. Embrace your inner most optimism and make your dreams come true. Go Team You!

Baking is a science and if you put too much of one ingredient or too little, your gourmet masterpiece can turn out to be a disaster. So many people tend to shy away from trying something new in their lives no matter how much they may crave it. Everyone can bake, as long as they have the right tools. Just like baking, we can all "do" life. All we need are the right ingredients and utensils. God has provided us with the recipe book to follow, we just need to read it, not be timid or fearful of messing things up and make something fabulous out of our lives! Go Team You!

I hate making my bed but when it's not made, the entire room APPEARS to be in disarray. When we create messes in our lives, sometimes instead of taking the time to straighten them out we ignore them and go on our merry way. Unfortunately, the messes we make, like the unmade bed, will be waiting for us upon our return. Deal with your issues! Don't just pull the covers over the problem because underneath the problem will still persist. My mom used to tell my dad," the last one up makes the bed." WELL JESUS IS ALWAYS UP FIRST BUT HE WILL HELP YOU TUCK IN THE SIDES. Go Team You!

So you are smiling and profiling, sitting on top of the world!! You're not just picking up yardage but in spite of blocks and attempts to tackle you to the ground, you have actually scored a touchdown or two (or three). Then just as you think you are unstoppable, the LIGHTS GO OUT!! Something beyond your control alters the course that you were on. You begin to start losing ground and it feels that you will never get back to where you were before. Do you throw up your hands and give up or do you fight for what you believe is yours regardless of the adversity that faces you?! Your quarterback is in place, He has called out the play, go get your super bowl ring! Go Team You!

Did you know…Humpty dumpty had a great fall! Make up your mind already and stop sitting on the fence (or in Humpty's case the "wall"). Humpty's biggest issue was that he only had "all the kings horses and his men" to put him back together again but you actually have the King of Kings! So it's okay if you fall because He will pick up the pieces. So stop sitting on the fence regarding that decision you have been putting off forever! Go for it and don't worry if you fall because He's got you! Go Team You!

It's a" row, row, row your boat," type of day. Have you ever rowed a boat? It takes some skill to navigate the boat and you must exert some energy. If you decide not to row you leave your fate up to the body of water that you are in…which means you can simply float with no direction or you can be carried away against your will and end up somewhere you don't want to be. The nursery rhyme ends with the consequences of rowing…"life is but a dream." Your choice. Go Team You!

Did you do something recently that you knew was wrong? Had you done it before? Will you do it again? History repeats itself because we CHOOSE to repeat it!! When children throw rocks and break a window, we scold them and perhaps we send them to TIME OUT so they can contemplate their actions and the consequences. If they go out and repeat the negative behavior the punishment becomes more severe. When we take over from our parents and self-punish we tend to forgive, justify and simply ignore our negative actions which leads to repeat offenses. So the next time you throw a rock through a window put yourself in time out and review, repent and reposition yourself so not to REPEAT again! Go Team You!

vegetables and jams, then preserve them in mason jars to be shared with family, friends and anyone that was in need. As God's mason jars He filled us up with the perfect mix of ingredients, so when the time is right we can open up to those that need us and the goodness inside can be shared. Are you sharing what was placed perfectly inside of you? If not, why not? Like the contents of the Mason jar, it was not meant to remain inside indefinitely. Eventually the flavors dissipate and lose their appeal. Don't allow your purpose to dissipate or lose appeal; share the flavors that only you encapsulate. Go Team You!

Stop pushing the snooze button when it comes to your life!!
GOD has set an alarm just for you! He wants you to wake up
from your slumber of complacency so that you can fulfill your
PURPOSE! Don't roll over and ignore it. Time is passing and
for every minute that you snooze that is a minute that you can
never recover. You have slept long enough, GET up now and
MAKE A DIFFERECE IN YOUR FUTURE! Go Team You!

So often, we get stuck in our daily routines that we don't take the opportunity to "live." This life is short so we can't wait to start living it...it's time to just do "it!" Whatever "it" is. May it be chasing your dreams, changing your environment or something as small as going to a concert on a Monday night, it's time to come out of your comfort zone and make the most of this precious thing called life before you are a day too late. Go Team You!

What do you do when temptation calls your name?! It could be as small as eating something that YOU KNOW YOU SHOULDN'T CONSUME or or DOING something THAT YOU KNOW YOU WILL REGRET later. Yet we allow temptation to cover our eyes finding no fault with living for the moment and comfortably forgetting about the consequences of our actions. How about today, we look into our crystal ball and contemplate what will be the result of our giving into the things that call our names in the dark? I'm thinking if we do, we can bask in the light with a clear mind and heart! Go Team You!

It is said there is a time and season for people in our lives, which is an extremely difficult concept to grasp when people that love us leave or in contrast when people that hurt us seem to linger like a piece of bubble gum stuck to your shoe on a hot day in July. Nothing happens by accident, life experiences, painful or pleasurable are on purpose, God's purpose. So learn from those who share even a moment of your life, they are there for a reason. Go Team You!

Yesterday I was driving and talking on my phone to a young man trying to start his career seeking advice. Within a blink of an eye, I almost lost my life as a car was speeding out of control and almost fatally hit me. It is by the grace of God that I got to see another day. Since my incident, a few things have tested me and I have fallen short of my keeping it all together. So I am taking a breath, pausing a moment to thank God and putting "it" all into perspective. There was a chance that my children could have lost me yet I am still here, so does the other stuff really matter? Just think about it and decide to make this day matter.

Go Team You!

One weekend, my youngest, Claudia, was attacked by a stomach virus and it was all hands on deck cleaning up the trail of what hurricane Claudia left behind (sorry if you haven't eaten)! There was one exception, and that was Zack, my 14 year old. He refused to be near her or help clean up after her! He was avoiding her like the plague!! Needless to say it he caught the virus within 24 hours of Claudia (it also hit my other daughter at 2:30am, so I was a busy bee). You can't avoid life. It will happen. You can't run from the situations that make you uncomfortable or unhappy. You have to take life on as it comes and pray for strength and in my case a strong stomach!!! It's not unicorns and rainbows all the time but you do control how you cope when not so good things happen. BREATHE, PRAY AND KEEP MOVING! HAVE A FANTABULOUS DAY ON PURPOSE!!! Go Team You!

"Don't miss your time, don't miss your season, don't miss your purpose!" Don't go through another day with your eyes wide shut! No day is disposable therefore, no day is a Robotic day. Don't just switch on the "on" button and methodically just "get through" the day...make your everyday a day worth living. This is your time and season, so fulfill your purpose! Go Team You!

In Spanish the term, "Vale la pena" means, "is it worth it?" When we intentionally hurt someone because they hurt us first-is it Vale la pena? When we share someone's secret-is it Vale la pena? When we know something or someone is not good for us but we don't let go - is it Vale la pena? That last piece of chocolate cake - is it Vale la pena? Uh…YES, I think so!!! Go Team You!

TIP TOE THROUGH THE TULIPS (BUT DON'T STEP ON THEM BECAUSE THEY COST TOO MUCH TO REPLACE)! Have you ever found yourself somewhere that you shouldn't be and it ended up costing you? The cost could end up being a financial, physical or emotional bind. You end up paying a high price for a situation that you could have avoided. You knew in your gut that you should have backed away but you ignored the warnings that clearly stated "don't step here" and you decided to take your chances. It is never too late to right a wrong, back away and ask for forgiveness. Pray for support and next time watch where you are stepping. Go Team You!

External factors, people and issues, can find a way into our psyche and setup business! These factors may not intend to be negative but once they enter our already over-crowded life, they become like a thief in the night and steal our joy! Well the time has come for us to police our own minds and hearts. DON'T LET THEM IN! Stop the issues and people at the door!! You and you alone have the power to decide how someone or something is going to impact you!! If you need to call in the reinforcements, drop down on your knees and look up!!! Save yourself! Go Team You!

"WATCHA WANNA" SAY? Well, spit it out. You were not given a spirit of fear so if you have something to say, why not say it? Are you fearful of the response? Are you weary of how you will be looked at or perceived? What are you actually gaining by not saying what's on your mind? There is a time to be quiet and simply listen but there is also a time to say what is weighing on your heart before the moment is gone forever. Don't hush your spirit when your soul wants to shout! Go Team You!

Why are waiting for the perfect mate, job situation and/or financial environment? That's like holding your breath under water and treading. Eventually you stop breathing and you cease living. You no longer are enjoying the moment and you miss out on present opportunities because you are looking pass them. Have faith that tomorrow will come but breathe, enjoy and live today!! Go Team You!

Last night I sat down with my ex and apologized for my role in the demise of our marriage. I was a big girl and took responsibility for my actions AND WHY NOT!? I made resolutions, laid the foundation for a new, and improved me! And WHY NOT!!!? It's TIME! No MORE EXCUSES! Everyday we go to work, school or whatever our thing is but what are we really doing? Are we taking responsibility, laying foundations, keeping promises, DOING OUR BEST...? If not, WHY NOT?! Go Team You!

Us plus silence equals a dark place. Often we engulf ourselves in noise because the silence is too loud - TV, music, texting, calls, just anything so we don't have to face the silence which may lead us to a dark place within our thoughts. There is a saying that "silence is golden". It is time for us to face what hides in the darkness. Shed light on it and find peace within it. You are not alone so don't be afraid. Turn off the noise. Go Team You!

I'm not the only indecisive person out here. I am not the only one that wants to be able to have their cake, pie, steak and eat them too! Yet there comes a time when we have to mature, cut loose the things, people and or concepts that are just not good for us. You know what I'm talking about and you can't continue to justify those things and or people anymore! Make a stand. No, it will not be easy but yes, it will be worthwhile. I PROMISE!!!
Go Team You!

Yesterday I had an interesting discussion with friends about the desire to control every aspect of one's life and not knowing when or how to relinquish that control. Wisdom comes when you realize that although every vessel has a Captain it also has a second in command. There are times in our lives that we are not meant to direct the excursion and if we don't relinquish the wheel, an iceberg may be our fate. Recognize when to step aside, humble yourself and learn from others. The destination is set, enjoy the journey. Go Team You!

. WAITING on the storm, ANTICIPATING the worse, WONDERING how we will cope and PONDERING why? Why do we sit around WAITING for a storm instead of enjoying the sun that is presently warming our souls? Why do we ANTICIPATE Armageddon instead of hoping for the best? And why WONDER how we will cope in a storm, since we are never really alone, are we? Weathering life's storms only makes us stronger and more reliant on our Storm Protector. So stop waiting, anticipating, and wondering. You will survive the storm. Go Team You!

"Time for bed sleepy head," "but I'm not sleepy yet!" As children we don't want to go to sleep because we feel that we may miss something; as adults we can't sleep because there is too much "something" that still needs to be done and as we mature sleep takes over no matter what we do!! Sleep is a time to rest and rejuvenate our entire beings. There has to be a time, daily, where we have to turn off the world around us and simply be quiet "sleep mode." We don't actually have to go to sleep but we must take time to rest and shut out the noise outside and inside our heads. Let the stresses that bind us be released and find solace in a moment. You need it. Go Team You!

When making edits to a document the "track changes" option allows you to see the original text as well as the changes that are suggested to improve the document. Now as the drafter, you can either accept or reject the changes. When accepting the changes to the document you must consider two things: who is suggesting the edits and what impact they will have? Therefore, you must not allow just anyone to take on the role of editor. There is One that I would recommend to you, He is the Master Editor and you can rest assure that all the changes he suggests are necessary and the final draft will be better than anything you could imagine.
Go Team You!

Like Popeye, we all get beat up once in awhile and need help to defeat the enemy or overcome an obstacle. Unlike Popeye, we silently suffer, cry alone or hold large pity parties for ourselves rather than admit to anyone that we are vulnerable, needy or just want someone near. When Bluto got the best of our hero, Popeye called out for help to obtain his spinach which was usually out of his reach. He was never too proud to ask for assistance. He let down his guard and admitted that he was infallible (we all are). Call out for help when you need it, God is standing by with your can of spinach, it maybe in the form of a friend co-worker or family member. Your only job is to be ready and willing to receive it. Go Team You!

Oh my goodness! There is nothing more irritating than a small speck in your eye. You can't ignore the irritation. You ask someone to blow in it, you wash it out and you stare in the mirror blinking until it is removed and the relief is unbelievable. There is something going on in your life right now that is just as irritating. You may be trying to ignore it but it is impacting you. Ask for help to remove it, examine it, decide the best way to eliminate the obstruction and most importantly pray on it because the relief once it's gone will be unspeakable! Have a great day because you choose to. Go Team You!

Are you okay? People ask us daily "how are you?" and many times we answer automatically and for the most part we don't answer "I am fabulous", marvelous" or even just "great"! Isn't that a pity? We busy ourselves daily and hide ourselves behind tasks and the daily grind sometimes as an escape and other times because we have grown so accustomed to not taking a moment for ourselves. So today, I challenge you to take a moment and ask yourself, "how am I doing?" And if you don't like the answer and even if you do, take another moment and pray. Go Team You!

I have ridden a donkey in the Sahara, swam in the Mediterranean, parasailed in Boracay (won't do that again, ugh) and eaten cat in Sri Lanka! Why? Because God has secured me with all the necessary equipment to live this life to the fullest and then he handed me a bungee cord made of blessings. Now my opportunities may not be your opportunities (like moving to Mexico and eating scrub worm tacos) but they exist if you open your eyes. So with my eyes wide open, I never say "no" when Jesus says "jump"...and neither should you! Go Team You!

I'm from NJ so I know what snow is. I heard in passing that there was a chance for snow and guess what? IT IS WINTER!! Even with all those factors, I didn't prepare and NOW THERE IS SNOW OUTSIDE. Sometimes we are fully aware of the pitfalls that lay ahead of us and we have many opportunities to avoid them YET WE FALL ANYWAY with our eyes wide open!! Next time u see the cliff ahead and you are running toward it at top speeds u should PREPARE to PREVENT yourself from going over and then simply PRAY! Go Team You!

Then the wolf cried, "I'll HUFF AND I'LL PUFF..." and the first and second little piggies trembled in their designer boots because they knew their homes, while aesthetically beautiful, had no foundation and if one true disaster landed at their doorstep their homes would never be the same! Now we ALL know what happened in the story, the third little piggy had built his house on a solid foundation and no matter the turmoil that ensued outside his home, he was protected inside. Do you have the solid foundation NEEDED TO STAND UP AGAINST THE WOLVES THAT HOWL OUTSIDE YOUR DOOR? If not, it is time to rebuild! Go Team You!

"Time Will Heal All"...Will it? Have you let go of the disappointment, hurt and/or sadness that was dumped on you by another a long, long time ago? Or does it actually linger in the hidden closet of your soul waiting for that perfect quiet moment which quickly turns dark when it pops out of its hiding place like a jack-in-box. What impact is this hurt having on your life? It is time to clean out the closet. Molly Maid may not live with you but Jesus does.   Who else can go into the dark and heal the hurt? Don't allow another day to go by that you don't call on Him to battle what hides in the shadows of your existence. Go Team You!

The uncertainty of the storm has passed, we survived and a new day is dawning. Coming out of a deep sleep, tucked- in snuggly like a child and despising the alarm ringing that interrupts all that is comforting, comfortable and tantalizing. Now the sobering reality…it's a new day, filled with new opportunities, challenges and a chance for us to triumph over all that defeated us yesterday!!! Thank God for what you will face today. The glory is His and the satisfaction is yours. Go Team You!

.

What have you talked yourself out of lately? Did you want to pick up the phone and call or text someone but then you THOUGHT about it and decided against it? Perhaps that person needed to hear from you. Did you want to do or say something but you THOUGHT about it and decided it wasn't necessary? Perhaps it could have made a difference in your day, or even in your life. We were blessed with the ability to reason, so there are instances that we should take our time and think things out BUT NOT ALL THE TIME. Sometimes we think too long and we get it wrong. Trust your gut, your instincts and live a little.
Go Team You!

In Jack and the Beanstalk, Jack got the goose that laid the golden eggs because he took on the Giant that stood in his way. What is your goose and what is the obstacle that is hindering you from obtaining it? Perhaps to answer that question you simply have to look in the mirror and ask yourself the question, are you the Giant that is blocking your way back home? If so, GET OUT OF THE WAY AND GET WHAT'S YOURS...And live HAPPILY EVER AFTER. Go Team You!

:

Corn stalk mazes- LOVE THEM!!!! During the fall, my children and I go to harvest festivals and we ALWAYS visit the corn maze. As we enter, we are usually giggling, bumping into one another and bubbling over with anticipation regarding what we have gotten ourselves into. Half way through, we have run into enough dead ends that our giggling excitement has waned, a little panic has set in and our minds start to wander to a place called "what would happen if we can't find our way out of here?!?" There is an ending to the maze and if you can't find your way out on your own, you can always follow someone to the exit. Are you lost in a maze of confusion (i.e. job issue, relationship, family dispute, self-imposed mess)? When you entered into it you were excited but somewhere along the lines you ran into dead ends? It is time to put on your big boy/girl pants and find your way out and if you have difficulty call on and follow HIM to the exit! Go Team You!

Doesn't the idea of fish fried hard served with cabbage, candied yams and cornbread put a smile on your face? When I wake up in the morning I'm always planning my next meal and don't let a holiday be on the horizon because everything must stop until I figure out what I will be serving. We need to find things in life (outside of food) that put a smile on our face, which we can plan for, implement and execute with ease. We need to find something outside of work, family and chores that define who we are and make a difference. With a new day on the horizon (called tomorrow) take this moment to enhance your life and find something that will feed your soul! Go Team You!

Love me tender, love me true. Are we truly lovable? Would you want to date or be married to someone like you? If not, why not? I believe to be truly lovable; we must begin by loving ourselves. Yes, we have flaws, imperfections and some bad habits but we are each a unique creation, molded by the hands of the Almighty, therefore we are worthy of love. Now, with that in mind, remember too, that your partner of choice is also an imperfect creation. So accept and love them for who they are not for who you hope they will become. Love doesn't have to be complicated and becoming lovable is just about removing all the "stuff" that masks who you really are. Go Team You!

Can Friday be MY DAY, please??? NO, NO, N-O! Isn't it hard to imagine that such a small word can change the course of your life? Many of us are allergic to it and if we say it we go into convulsions and others of us learned the word at age two and can't stop saying it. For those of us whose throats get dry and close up at the thought of telling someone no, this day is for you! Save yourself, your sanity, your time and say, "no" today! Don't feel guilty about putting your wants, needs and desires first. Love you today and make it a "my" day. Go Team You!

Fixodent and forget it! What a catchy tag line for denture cream and what a novel concept. In reality, is there anything you can fix and forget? Perhaps temporarily but not indefinitely. Everything from a mended chair to a mended heart needs to be cared for and eventually mended again. If you have been fortunate enough to fix a broken relationship with a friend, family member, or love interest don't leave it to chance and forget about it. Nurture it, coax it along and continue to work on it. If you haven't fixed that broken relationship yet, consider reaching out to that person today, not just for their sake but for yours as well. We all need the sense of being whole in the pursuit for peace. Forgive and be forgiven. Go Team You!

Someone once told me that when putting the past into perspective in your life to think of yourself driving a car. The windshield is large so you can see where you are going (and your options for how you want to get there). Yet the rearview mirror is small because where you just came from is much less important. Some of us get so caught up in looking back in the rearview, that we end up going nowhere, having accidents or getting lost!! It is imperative that every so often we glance back to ensure no one behind us is going to cause us any issues; to check that the coast is clear when we are ready to change lanes and also just to remember where we came from. Other than that, belt yourself in, adjust the mirrors, face forward and drive! Go Team You!

Jesus is the reason for the season and HE equals LOVE! SO don't worry about spending money on gifts u can't afford, or not being able to be with family and friends or sad just because. This is a time to give the most precious gift of all and that is your love. May u be near or far, let those close to you know that they are loved and more importantly know that you're loved and never alone!!!! Go Team You

We interrupt your regular Monday morning routine for the following announcement: THERE'S A DELAY!!! I sincerely appreciate the local and federal governments' precautionary measures which results in delays and closures. We, on the other hand, can't afford to do the same! When the storms of our lives dump 5 feet of worries and obstacles at our door, we must not delay our progress!!! We must get out our shovel of determination and plow ahead!!! Please stay safe during the storm! Go Team You!

"What you won't do, you'll do for love," not just lyrics to my favorite song but words to love by. Romeo and Juliet understood the concept. Samson got the memo even though Delilah deleted it when it hit her inbox. Unfortunately, many of us didn't sit through the seminar and refuse to read the Cliff Notes. In this microwavable society where everything must be immediate, some things, like Love, should take time, effort and deliberate commitment. Who said that love HAD to be rainbows and butterflies? Who said that love had to reside in YOUR comfort zone and YOUR happy place in order for it to flourish? What you won't do you, can, should and better - do for love! Go Team You!

Do you know your mission? We were not created to serve our own needs. We were put here to make a difference! You have been given Purpose and you are the only one who can fulfill it!

Look outside of yourself and all that consumes you. Ask yourself why are you here? You may already know and living a life that is making an impact but if you don't know, take the time to figure it out. The mission is not impossible because you were made to do great things. Don't waste another minute of your life not living out your destiny. Go Team You!

"Once a task is first begun never leave it until it's done. May the task be great or small do it well or not at all! "Would you hit a baseball out of the park and stop running when you got to second base? Then why haven't you completed that task, wrapped up that DIY project you started last year and/or finished that class? Whatever "it" is, you started "it" with the idea that you would be better off once you completed "it" SO WHAT HAPPENED? Close your eyes and imagine this: the crowd is cheering you on, the smell of hot dogs is in the air, the pitcher throws a fastball, you hit a grand slam...don't stop on second base, RUN HOME! Go Team You!

"Today on the Dr. Val show we have Mr. Big Bad Wolf who starred in that family favorite Little Red Riding Hood." "Mr Wolf has come to us today wanting to know what he could have done differently so he, too, could have realized his Happily Ever After." "Well, Mr. Wolf it is as simple as saying "Little Red, I'm sorry that I deceived you." "Please forgive me if I hurt you, Grandmother." "Be assured in knowing that it is never too late to right a wrong, for Mr. Wolf or for any of us. Humbling oneself is not a sign a weakness but a sign of integrity and strength." "Now, Mr. Wolf, pack a picnic basket and invite your new friends to spend some quality time together!" Go Team You!

You will never guess what I saw yesterday! I am not one to gossip but I have to share... A woman stepped out of her car, STOPPED, bent down and literally smelled the roses!! Who does that? So many of us are stuck on fast forward times 3! Intentionally? Probably not. Personally, I have become like Donald Trump, constantly trying to figure out my next move; Molly Maid always trying to clean up my last mess (figuratively and literally) and Dr. Phil, self diagnosing the last crazy thing I did and still trying to figure out WHY. So when do I get to "stop and smell the roses?" Right NOW because tomorrow isn't promised and the beauty of the day is waiting to be acknowledged. Go Team You!

If you were offered the opportunity to travel back into time, would you go?   Would you choose a happy time to visit or a time of struggle and strife? Sometimes I wonder if I am truly forgetful or is it simply easier not to remember. All memories are not pleasant but in order to proceed forward we must pay homage, find peace with and be grateful that we made it through the past. On Memorial Day we remember the fallen soldiers, we remember what they sacrificed for reasons we may never know but we know that their choices could not have been easy. Remember to thank God for the past, painful and pleasant. Take the opportunity to travel back into time so you can face it, fix what you can and, learn from it. Go Team You!

Choo choo! The train is boarding let's get on!!! There is so much to see in the world, don't miss it! Life is waiting for you! Plane, boat, train, car... whatever the mode of transportation, no matter the destination it is time to change the scenery! Open yourself up to new experiences, fun, laughter and life!! I got my ticket do you have yours! Go Team You!

When we left our story sweet little Goldilocks had just been
discovered sleeping in Baby Bear's bed after she had spent the
entire morning trying out all of the family's chairs looking for the
"perfect" seat. She then spent lunch tasting everyone's porridge
until she found one that was "perfect" for her palate. Sleepy from
the morning events she sought out the "perfect" bed. So here we
are now... frightened for her life she flees from the Bear's home
barely able to breathe! So what's the moral of the story? Stop
seeking perfection!! There comes a time when you should
simply appreciate what is in front of you. If Goldilocks had
done just that, she could have eaten and taken a nap before the
Bear family even returned home!!!! Go Team You!

Throw it away? Give it away? Sell it? Pass it down? When George and Weezie moved to the deluxe apartment on the East Side do you think they faced the same moving issues I faced when I moved to MD? The most difficult part of moving on, is letting go, separating and walking away from the past. There are the memories, the keepsakes, the always and forevers... There comes a time when decisions have to be made and some things in our lives must be left behind. So choose carefully and you too can be "moving on up!" Go Team You!

"Please take the Safety Information Card out of the seat pocket in front of you..." how many times have you heard that?! You feel like you can recite it, right? But would we know what to do in the case of a "real" emergency?! Would we remember to blow in the tube on the vest or to follow the floor lights to the nearest exit? We need to stop tuning out what we consider the background noise in our lives. People are positioned in our day-to-day, to guide, lead and protect us (sometimes from ourselves) so let's listen. Go Team You!

"Think long, think wrong!" How many things have you talked yourself out of, just this week alone? How many opportunities slipped through your fingers as you sat analyzing the pros and cons? Not every decision in your life has to be dissected like the frog in your 5th grade science class. Trust your instincts to guide you through this maze of life. If you get lost, so what... that is part of the adventure.   If you get hurt, it is okay you will heal! Stop over thinking and start living over! Go Team You!

Did you hear? Mother Nature is missing!!! I knew something was wrong when I woke up on a beautiful May morning, put on a lovely spring dress and walked outside to 40 degree weather!

We come to expect some things to be the same in our lifes forever. So when life's puzzle pieces don't fall into place we get out the "make it work" scissors to make them fit. Sometimes people are not going to behave the way we expect and things don't always happen the way they have in the past. Do we throw up our hands and turn our back on life when it changes without our permission? No!! We will adjust, adapt and put on an overcoat!! Go Team You!

It's either my way or the highway!! You may have never said or thought those words but your actions may have screamed them!!

At age nine, my daughter was intuitive enough to buy me a bracelet that says "you can agree with me, or you can be wrong." What a sad, but true commentary about many of us. We believe what we say is fact and we will argue our point to the death. As the years pass, I realize more and more how much I don't know. I welcome others' opinions and guidance in life. I am wrong (at times) and humbly admit it. Do you? Go Team You!

What not to wear -- the cloak of invisibility! You were created to be seen, heard and your impact felt. When getting dressed daily remember to always dress for success. This goes beyond your clothing. To be seen, hold your head high because you are a child of the Almighty. To be heard, speak words of positivity to those who seek your advice. To make an impact, hone your gifts and share them with the world. Go Team You!

"Beep! Beep!" The Roadrunner zips by with Wile E Coyote in hot pursuit until..."BANG! "an anvil, piano, house or something falls on poor Coyote. Yes, I said "poor" Coyote because apparently, he's hungry and I guess McDonald's missed putting a franchise out in the desert. So the Coyote keeps his eyes on the prize!! He is my HERO!! A role model for us all! He is determined, steadfast and focused on his goal regardless of the obstacles that fall on him along the way. Don't let an anvil stand between you and your goal! Dig deep and find the Coyote in you, because nothing beats a failure but a try --"Beep! Beep!" Go Team You!

Sticks and stones may break my bones BUT NAMES CAN, DO and WILL cause permanent damage, especially those sent by text! In this age of texting, we sometimes become too comfortable in substituting a text message for a phone call. I understand the convenience aspect but I also know that text messages can be misinterpreted and lead to bad feelings, hurt egos and yes, even to the brink of break ups! When a serious matter needs to be discussed or when a line of texting turns the wrong way down a one way street it is time to make a call. Old fashion? Maybe. Priceless? Most definitely! Go Team You!

What do you want? Do you know? How do you pursue your heart's desires if you have not identified what they are? You can't start the race if you don't know where the finish line is! Decide what it is you want, pray about it, make a plan to obtain it, then go get it!! Is it that easy? Of course not but if you really want it nothing else should matter. Go Team You!

Valerie's Traveling to Taiwan Tip #105 - When attending a business lunch or dinner be prepared to consume a large amount of food. The meals are served family style on a lazy Suzie. An interesting tidbit about the dining experience in Taiwan is that a CEO of a major company or a member of congress could be serving you the duck! Regardless of their position, title and/or bank account, the Taiwan people will serve those next to them before serving themselves. No one is too good to serve (or help) someone else. That person's goal is to ensure the happiness of their companion before their own. Looking out for those around you is a noble exercise. It doesn't take much from you to be thoughtful in your actions. Make a difference today in someone else's life by serving up a better you. Tip #106 Don't Gan Bei!
Go Team You!

Small print "geesh! " As soon as we returned to the States, I bought one of those monstrosities of a TV that did everything short of my laundry. Before I could learn how to turn it on my darling son put a small hairline crack in it which meant the end before the beginning. Oh well. At least I had purchased the warranty so if it anything went wrong I would be covered, right? WRONG!!! "Screens not covered" that apparently was the small print. Small print is found in most binding agreements with one exception that I know of first hand, when you agree to put the Lord first in your life you are loved unconditionally, NO SMALL print!! Go Team You!

Last night a friend of mine told me that he was "waiting" on his blessing and I told him he was already living it. How many of us forget that fact? As I lie here in my bed (yes, I'm off from work today! Thank God!) the sun is shining and the birds are singing all I want to do is say "Thank you" for my life which is a blessing!! From the roof over my head, to the love of my daughter who just hugged me. What more could I want? If that wasn't enough, I have fabulous friends and food in my refrigerator!! When you are feeling low, remember that you are loved by the Almighty and if you can't see it, open your eyes and look around. Go Team You!

"Ladies and Gentlemen, we are beginning our descent and we'll be landing on the island of Excuse very shortly." "The Captain wanted me to remind you of a few housekeeping items before we land." The island is covered with the "I Can't" bug. If bitten by one it will leave you incapacitated. We also suggest you don't visit the "Amen Corner." "Many badly afflicted residents of Excuse Island setup camp on this corner looking for new recruits." "Our final recommendation from The Captain is DON'T DEBOARD THE PLANE!!" "We are offering full refunds and vouchers to any passengers looking to try a different destination." "There are still flights available to Optimisim and Hope, book your tickets TODAY!" Go Team You!

What does Snow, Beast, Cindy, Beauty and you have in common? Oh come on you know! "HAPPILY EVER AFTERS" of course! Like Shrek, we have drama, crazy friends, problems with our loved ones, sometimes we may even wish for a different life but just like the ogre, at the close of each movie, or in our case at the close of each "chapter" in our lives, we realize that we HAVE BEEN living our "HAPPILY EVER AFTER (HEA)" What do you mean, you didn't notice? It is all relative, there is no Perfect life but we can be happy with the blessed life we are living it is up to you. Put on your HEA glasses and have a smile. Go Team You!

When I was at my Father's knee, he began to teach me about responsibilities. Living a life that was carefree was over for me around age three. Here was His plea, which at the time sounded very simple to me: "do unto others as you would have them do unto thee!" As an adult that is so difficult, you see, because not everyone learned that decree, but it is our job to stay true to the One that holds Heaven's key! Go Team You!

Picture this, my family, which at any time can include anywhere from 5-50 people (we are a loving bunch), in beautiful Amsterdam on bikes searching for windmills (just call me Love Boat Julie because I'm always planning some crazy outing)! After 5 hours of peddling and no windmill sightings, we determined we were lost (apparently map reading was easier in grammar school)! It was a "loving life sunshiny kind of day," the kind that reminds you that sometimes the journey is more important than the destination! So take-in the sights and enjoy the journey that you are traveling on today, the windmills may come tomorrow. Go Team You!

Here today and forever gone tomorrow. I was cheerfully rambling on with a colleague on Friday about absolutely nothing (I do that). The sun was shining, the birds were chirping and it was Friday! On Saturday morning, I opened my eyes, stretched and I was blessed to face another day but she was not. We all understand the concept of the inevitable but when it knocks on your door and enters you begin to pay attention. On her last Friday, she smiled, she laughed, she looked forward to, and she had hope for a better tomorrow. Isn't that how we should all live every day? Go Team You!

There was an old woman who lived in a shoe. She was so overwhelmed she didn't know what to do! "Go to Zumba," I said "or spend the day in the bed!" "But I can't!" she cried "the car battery just died, my project is due and little Sally stepped in doggy poo!" "What a mess! But you've done your best, so it's time to hit the clearance rack at Nine West!" How will I end this you wonder, I too began to ponder and decided I could no longer rhyme (it's 4 am!). So here is the moral: take some time for yourself because everything will still be there tomorrow! Go Team You!

Today is a new day, so GET ON YOUR MARK by choosing what you will conquer this God given day! Now GET SET! What do you need to shift, change, adapt, compile and/or simply "do" to prepare yourself? Yes, there may be hurdles, leg cramps and the sun may become intense but the COACH has trained you to handle any obstacle that you may face! So don't allow the fear of defeat beat you before you even begin! Ready or not...GO! Do it! No "ands, ifs or buts." The race has started don't get left at the starting line!! Go Team You!

Click click, click! Your heart begins to beat faster, your hands begin to sweat, your mind races! OMG! What am I doing here? " click! CLICK!! Here we go!!! YAY! It is time to enjoy this ride we call "LIFE!" Every up, down, loop, and turn we should embrace and absorb the impact because every emotion we experience makes this ride worth living. Who would we be if we didn't FEEL it all? So buckle up, throw your hands up, squeal with delight (even if it is just on the inside) and enjoy the ride because God's got this! Go Team You!

Now I lay me down to sleep...2:53am, I tossed. 3:20am I turned, 4:15am, I sighed. Stressed? Never! Simply Over stimulated!! In the quiet darkness of the early morning so many of us desire the Sandman to grace us with his presence but instead we are taunted by the thoughts of what we forgot to do, what we need to do and what we know we will forget to do!! How do we rest when our minds are in such turmoil? Breathe, Pray and Believe...the sun will rise and we will survive. Go Team You!

Good day and welcome to our seminar "Positivity, a Myth? I think Not!" Today we will study a day in the life of ...wait for it...a fly! Glamorous? No! A symbol of positive endurance? Yes!   Wherever the fly lands it makes the most out of it, may it be a dump or Aunt Sylvia's potato salad! The fly can be swatted, shood away or sprayed but it will come back again and again 'til it gets what it needs. Learn from the fly to get what you need from every situation no matter the obstacles! Go Team You!

An insatiable hunger is one that is impossible to satisfy. This can be a positive endeavor or maybe not. YOU know if your obsession has taken the wrong turn at the fork in the road. You continue to feed it what YOU believe it wants, when in reality it may be the outcome of a deeper rooted issue. Do you have an insatiable appetite? It could be for something intangible such as attention, pity, and/or love or it could be tangible like cigarettes, books or food. Is it a hunger that you want to continue to feed because it nourishes who you are or is it a fattening negative pursuit which is creating a glutton that is overtaking who you want to be? If the latter, change your diet. Go Team You!

The EXCUSE: "He's hurt." "She's tired.""He doesn't know what he did.""She didn't mean to say that." The REALITY: You didn't hurt him, so why should you suffer. She's NOT tired just cranky. He DOES know what he did. She DID mean to say it. Stop making excuses for others' behavior. Many of us are blessed with a sound mind (some days it is more sound than others). We are equipped to make good choices, such as the option to NOT cause another person pain on purpose. Remember that when good sense is rejected, NO excuses SHOULD BE accepted! Go Team You!

The enemy is lurking in the shadows!!! Waiting, watching, scheming his next step! Patiently holding back until you are tired, weak and vulnerable. Yes, you will recognize him because you see him each time you look in the mirror! WE are our worse enemy!! No one, not even Satan himself can hurt us as much as we hurt ourselves. But have no fear, because able to create the world in 7 days is our Hero!! He is ready to drop everything and not just save the day but save us from ourselves!! He is waiting in the wings...simply call out His name and He will defeat what lurks in our darkness. Go Team You!

Shhhhh! Can you hear that? Well it appears that everyone around me can hear it, except me. It's my body talking. My eyes keep going behind my back and telling everyone that I'm tired. My mannerisms keep sharing my secret that I'm not feeling my best. For some reason I'm the only one not listening to my body as it complains of my maltreatment. I thought I heard a small voice last night saying "stop pushing me," but I couldn't be sure. I suppose I won't listen until I simply fall apart due to pure exhaustion!! Is your body talking? You may want to pay attention and heed its word...Watch me, I'm going back to bed (at least for 10 minutes). Go Team You!

When Fred couldn't stop the car, Barney threw his feet down. When Lucy couldn't wrap the chocolates fast enough, Ethel shoved them in her mouth. When Batman threw a right punch, Robin threw a left!! Do you have someone to help you put on the brakes when life is going too fast, to help you digest your problems and to fight besides you when the enemy attacks? An earthly sidekick is a blessing but if that person doesn't exist, or even if they do, never fear because Jesus is near. He will never forsake you. So when you are going thru, rest assure that you are never alone because He is your BFE (Best Friend for Eternity)! Go Team You!

Forget about the "lions, tigers and bears!" We've got the "boxes, anxiety and security deposits, OH MY!" Nothing is scarier than, MOVING!! The stress, the uncertainty, and the walk into the unknown, can all play havoc on your physical and mental well-being. Yet throughout the Bible, God had people moving to and fro because movement equals change, growth and opportunity. A move does not have to be as significant as changing locations, it can be as simple as changing your mindset. Walking down a path of life that you never had before. So let's not remain stagnate in our current reality, let's make a MOVE. Go Team You!

What do you imagine when you here the term "the morning after..." I picture some poor disheveled soul, cupping their head in their hands wishing they could turn back the hands of time. Have you ever felt the "morning after" disappointment in yourself? It's that moment when the light of reality shines on something "dark" that you said or did. It is the instant that the rays of regret illuminate upon what you've done that you want to hide and forget, but can't. The "morning after," is not only an awakening to the "oops" in the dark but it also represents a "new beginning." So ask for forgiveness, forgive yourself and enjoy a brand new day. Go Team You!

Stop, Hansel you SHOULDN'T trust her!!! Gretel DON'T eat that candy!!! Children, STOP indulging because YOU BELIEVE no one is watching!! Who (or what) are you allowing to fatten you up for the kill? You knew you SHOULDN'T go astray but you DIDN'T stop because you, too, wanted to indulge when you BELIEVED no one was watching! It is time to retreat before the oven gets too hot!!! If you forgot to leave the crumbs down to find your way home, No worries just follow His Word (you know Him, the One that is always watching!). Go Team You!

WATCH OUT!!!!! YOU'RE GOING TO FALLLLL!!!! Oh
No!!! You're broken!!!! Why so many pieces? You were broken
before and you tried to fix yourself? Oh, I see. You asked your
friends to help pick up the pieces but you were never the same?
Did you know that you are still under warranty? Yes, yes, you
are! If you return to the Original Manufacturer, He can repair
you and with the right tools and parts, you will be as good as
new. Oh, no need to thank me, that's what I'm here for! Go
Team You!

Someone said to me recently, "unless you interact with a person all you have is your perception of them." That goes back to the old saying "don't judge a book by its cover." Now raise your hand if you are guilty of doing just that (don't worry no one can see you and between you and me both my hands are raised!). My challenge to you today is to interact and dispel your perception of some special being. We are molded by our experiences and sometimes who we are, is not who we want to be, yet we are worth knowing. Precious are we created by He. Go Team You!

Did you hear? There was an eclipse this weekend!!!!! It happened the moment that my move took over my sunny disposition!!! Yes, I know that no one or nothing should ever steal my joy BUT after my 3rd day of moving from VA to MD my patience got misplaced somewhere between the elevator breaking down at 1am and me leaving my phone in the SECOND U-Haul truck I rented within 24 hours!! I felt as though there was a dark cloud that followed me from the time I drove the first raggedy truck until now as I sit with my oodles of noodles at 1am surrounded by the aftermath!! Then someone said to me what a successful move! Really? Yes, because of the outpouring of friends and family that came to help. Moral: Don't get so caught up in self-pity that you miss out on a blessing. Go Team You!

There are days when getting lost can be like an adventure and then there is today! After 4 days of moving, personal items MIA, sleep deprivation and confusion sticking to me like glue, the last thing I want or need is to get lost getting to the Metro train station which is 10 minutes from my home. While driving in circles (with a GPS, my fault not its), I attempted to rationalize what I was feeling but it didn't work!!! Do you ever feel lost, hopeless or just sad and no matter what you say or others say to you the feelings still linger? It's okay. What's not okay, is to stay lost! Call on your God that Provides Stability (GPS) to guide you to your destination! All is Never totally lost! Go Team You!

Aaaargh! Who puts garbage in a kitchen trash can that has no bag in it? My children, that's who!!!! So when I ask my "special" babies why they would do such a thing, they reply "because someone else did it first!!" Yikes!! So guilty of that one!! At times, we do things that make no sense at all but since others are doing it... Just because the garbage is already there doesn't justify us jumping in! Let's not be part of the problem (do what is right and go get a bag). Go Team You!

"Mommy, mommy, pleaseeee, mommy, please?" "No, you cannot jump off the roof, no, no, no." Sometimes saying "no," to our children is easy, especially when we know the consequences are detrimental. Unfortunately saying "no," to ourselves is a different story. We can be headed down a one-way street, on a motorcycle going backwards at top speeds with our hands tied and blindfolded and we will still tell ourselves that "it will be fine!" Let's not turn the common sense switch off when it comes to our own well-being...if we know the stove is hot, let's not touch it! No! Go Team You!

The knee bone is connected to the hip bone. The hip bone connected to the thigh bone. So what happened to the brain being connected to common sense?! On my good days, I can multiply, remember most of my grocery list when I'm at the store and call my children by their correct names but making a rational decision is as challenging as learning rocket science in Chinese!!! Is it that we lack the good sense gene? Nope!! Often we disconnect the brain's ability to make good sensible decisions by leaving God out of the equation and working off of "what feels good to us at the moment!" Oops! Time to reconnect "dem bones!" Go Team You!

"The first step to getting the things you want out of life is this: decide what you want." Ben Stein (1944). Sounds logical even simple but as you read this you began to ponder "have I ever TRULY, decided what it is that I want?" (Don't deny it, I saw you pondering). Sure, at some point we have all said those common phrases, "I wish..." "One day maybe..." "If only I had the time (money, energy etc...)..." You can't achieve if you don't believe and you can't believe in something you have never consciously decided you wanted!! Stop what you are doing right now and decide on what it is you want. Then go and get it (or at least get started trying to obtain it!!)! Go Team You!!

"Now I lay me down to sleep, I pray to God my soul to keep. If I should die before I wake I pray to God my soul to take."As a child, I said this prayer before I went to sleep and the concept of dying in my sleep frightened me. As an adult the prayer frightens me even more because the concept of sleep, for me, is no longer just the time that my eyes are shut and my body is at rest, it is my day-to-day status as I move around my life with my eyes open wide shut. Will I wake up and live the life God intended for me before departing this world? Will you? Go Team You!

I SAID IT!!!! I'm sorry!! I promised never to say that dirty four-letter word again, but it slipped out!!!!! I know, I was wrong but the time has come, AGAIN, for me to go on a D-I-E-T!!! Yes, I know the first three letters spell DIE but the concept is not bad. Think about it, when on a diet you make a conscious decision to cut things that are BAD for you out of your life. You become more aware of only putting GOOD stuff in that will make you a "better you," and in the end you feel better about who you are!!! Sorry, but I have to say it, (close your ears if you must) - maybe it's time you go on an emotional, physical or mental DIET TOO!!! Go TEAM YOU!!!

As a young child, the experience intimidated me. Even now as I think back on it I shudder. I can recall the unwelcome smell that slowly permeated my space as we entered, the dusk like darkness and the rising anxiety that took over my thoughts as I mentally hugged myself for reassurance. Sure, my parents sat up front chatting away but the car ride through the Holland Tunnel from NJ to NY was heart stopping. Although, I knew there was light, life and a fabulous city on the other side waiting for me, going through was difficult, scary and intimidating. Are you going through a tunnel and want to turn back? Perhaps you haven't even entered because you are fearful of the experience. My parents got me through but more importantly for you, OUR FATHER can drive you to your life on the other side if you relinquish the wheel. Don't be afraid. Find out what's at the other end of your tunnel. Go Team You!! Yay!

Good day, students and Welcome to Finance 101. Today's course is entitled "WHY IS THERE LENT AT THE BOTTOM OF YOUR POCKET!??!!" Hello? Yes, that was a question!! Whatever the current reason or excuse doesn't matter. Today is a NEW day and the first concept that we want you to grasp in this class is "Save a dollar, sleep ALL night!" Regardless of the amount of money that you earn YOU MUST SAVE something. Put it in the bank, shoebox, freezer, it doesn't matter just as long as you can become self-reliant, self-sufficient and well rested!! Homework: go do it now...SAVE!! Go Team You!!

Snow White SLEEP!!!" "She is exhausted!!!" "After the long commute to the forest, working all day at the Seven Dwarf's cottage and the meeting with that Apple seller, she needs a break!" Snow, like most of us, just won't stop going!! Overwhelmed with life and not knowing when to simply stop or just say "no" we go until we fall out from exhaustion! Let's take a "PAB" (Poison Apple Break) without the poison apple. Rest and rejuvenate!!! When you awaken, you too can live out the fairytale ending (at least until tomorrow!) Go Team You!! Yay!

Izzy Impatient needs a new license so she's headed to DMV.
Unfortunately, her attitude is poor before she hits the front door
because she expects the worse, and oops, she forgot the car key!!
Oh, Izzy dear, do not fear, no matter the lines you will be fine
because you are blessed! So what you will wait? Who cares
you'll be late? Let's focus on all that is great!! You can talk;
you are able to STAND in line and have a sound mind (I think!).
You woke up this morning to see another day so enjoy how you
spend it regardless the way because it's your and eventually, it
will go away! Go Team You!! Yay!!

"Those who stand for nothing fall for anything." OOPS!! Did you just stumble? Be careful!! As we all know, life is an obstacle course. Day after day, we are confronted with stumbling blocks disguised in the form of choices. When deciding between your choices, what or more importantly, WHO is your reference point? Are you making decisions willy nilly and if that's the case how is that working for you? Don't fret, I have a Bible for you to use as reference material and a first aid kit ready that you can borrow. Go Team You!

Hey!! How are you? I have a surprise for you!!! Close your eyes! Ready? Okay, here is the "Present" No need to thank me; Jesus bought it for you (with His life!). So are you going to put it to good use because you can't re-gift it? Please don't disregard it like you did with other "PRESENTS" FROM Him! Everyone didn't get one!! Please let Him know how grateful you are that He thought about you. Oh, you want to know how you can let Him know, short of a thank you card. It's simple, make the most out of the "PRESENT!" Go Team You!

It's a "my my Pinocchio the nose sure grows" day! Children sometimes lie to protect themselves when they have done something wrong or to embellish their lives to impress their peers. As adults, we sometimes tend to increase the amount of lies, not that we tell others but what we tell ourselves. We lie to ourselves about how we feel, our relationships, our skills, abilities or lack thereof. The lies can be damaging especially when we lie about who/what we are, what we really want and what we will accept. The only way Pinocchio could become a "real" boy was to tell the truth...don't you want to feel real? Go Team You!

OH NO!! WATCH OUT FOR THAT! Choo! Choo! Somewhere along my journey to destination "Getting it Together" I GOT DERAILED!!! Did I see the obstruction(s) that made me jump the track? Probably. Did I ignore them? Most definitely! Can I get back on track? OF COURSE I CAN AND SO CAN YOU!!! As the conductor of the 12:00am train to "Watch Out Here I Come," you have been EMPOWERED TO GET THAT TRAIN BACK ON TRACK. It doesn't matter how many times it derails just keep picking up the cargo that may have scattered and proceed full steam ahead. The little red caboose believed he COULD…and so should you! Go Team You!

"Where for art thou?" Perhaps that "special" person that you have been seeking has been right in front of you all along. That person that you have been wishing for to change your life, bring you happiness and make you feel complete, may be the one you saw when you looked in the mirror this morning when brushing your teeth! Outward love sometimes comes easier than the inward love that our souls thirst for… It is necessary to first and foremost love yourself and then receiving and recognizing others' "real" love can be effortless, exciting and everlasting. Go Team You!

No, no, I think it is too much to swallow! Don't choke! So often we bite off more than we can chew then we wonder why we are choking on life, suffering from indigestion and feeling bloated by issues. We must push back from the table and go on a drama-free diet. Learn to say "no." Exercise your right to take your time in every life situation. Don't feel pressured to move any faster than you are comfortable with. Slowly digest life and live. Go Team You!

Too little, too LATE?!? Never THAT! Do you want something but you have not put in enough time or effort so you have concluded that it will never be yours? Why not change your destiny and go after whatever you want TODAY??!! Don't give up and don't give in! Don't settle and NEVER BE CONTENT!!! Go for it!! DO IT!! Put your name on YOUR DREAM! It is never too late! Go Team You!

What are you missing? Like every morning on the Metro, yesterday I had my head down reading. For no apparent reason and contrary to the norm, I lifted my head and I experienced the most breathtaking sunrise. How often do I miss what is going on around me? We keep ourselves so busy at times that we miss the beauty that surrounds us. We get so caught up with "things" that we may miss the smile on our child's face, a friend needing to share a moment, an opportunity to experience happiness, or we could simply be busying ourselves with our "day to day" and miss a sunrise. Look up today and don't miss it...whatever "it" may be. Go Team You!

"WAKE UP, RIP!!!! Are you too tired to try, its only Thursday?" Rip Van Winkle slept for twenty years!!! Imagine how much he missed out on!! Have you ever experienced that moment when you say "where did the time go?" Let's call that a "Rip moment." Sometimes we sleepwalk through life going through the motions and forgetting to live! Let's abolish "Rip Moments" from our lives! WAKE UP AND PARTICIPATE IN AUTHORING YOUR NEXT ADVENTURE! Go Team You!

Forgive me…NOT!!! Now take a moment, think, ponder and dig deep before answering the questions that I will ask you. Are you ready? Have you EVER hurt someone? Did you ask for forgiveness or were you too proud to admit your mistake? Now turn that around, have YOU FORGIVEN THOSE who have caused damage in your heart, mind or total being? SOMETHING IS TO BE SAID FOR "treating others AS YOU WOULD LIKE TO BE TREATED." Let go and forgive someone today. You don't necessarily have to announce your action but start by letting it go silently within the confines of your heart. I promise that the day will become brighter. Go Team You!

Let's not repeat…SIMPLY DELETE!!! Ponder this thought for a moment…why do we cling to, repeat, hover around, refuse to let go, sit in, around, under and on top of things, people and/or behaviors that are, simply put, BAD for us? It's as if the Devil drops by for a visit and instead of making up the guest room, we give him the master suite!! Well, I challenge you today to delete the bad behavior, vices and/or people that have taken up residence in your life. Delete and deliver yourself from the bondage that keeps you from the happiness that you DESERVE!
Go Team You!

Totally, toasty, and Tucked-in…Awwwww. The uncertainty of
the storm has passed, we survived and a new day is dawning.
Coming out of a deep sleep, tucked- in snuggly like a child
and despising the ringing alarm that interrupts all that is
comforting, comfortable and tantalizing. Now the sobering
reality…it's a new day, filled with new opportunities, challenges
and a chance for us to triumph over all that defeated us
yesterday!!! Thank God for what you will face today. The glory
is His and the satisfaction is yours. Go Team You!

IT'S NOT FAIR! I want what I want when I want it - IMMEDIATELY, INSTANTANEOUSLY, RIGHT NOW!!! Why must I wait, exert effort, put in time or have to work for it? And when I can't get it when I want it or how I want it, I will walk away from it and pout, whine and complain."Ye of little faith." One must endure a little pain in order to achieve satisfaction. The reward is greater when effort, time and work are put forward. Go for what you want and be patient, it's worth the wait. Go Team You!

Tell me something good!! It takes no more energy to say something positive than to say something negative. Lifting someone up with your words can make their day, where saying something hurtful can linger for a lifetime. We don't always have to speak. Sometimes silence is our saving grace but our on/off switch gets stuck. You have the power to make someone's day, exercise that power! Go Team You!

Beware of the howling wind! I believe in what I cannot see. Last night the wind was so ferocious that I thought when I woke up this morning, I was going to find myself in Oz having landed on somebody's wicked witch! I could not see the wind but I shuddered at its howls. I felt its power and I feared its impact. The wind, although faceless to me, I recognized its presence. He who created the wind I have not seen but I shudder when He speaks to me. I have felt His power and His impact. Most importantly, I recognize His presence, although like the wind, I cannot see Him. **Go Team You!**

"What goes up must come down!" Sir Issac Newton's quote is based on the law of gravity. Unfortunately, for some of us it has become the law of life. We can't enjoy the "up" times of our lives because we are always waiting, anticipating and even looking for the "down" times around every corner. Guess what? It's okay to be happy. It's okay to laugh, smile and feel warm inside. It is okay to live. Yes, it may only last for a moment but you can string moments together and be grateful for these blessings. It is your choice. Do you simply want to reside in the "downs?" A dark dreary place of contentment OR will you Escape to the "ups" Resort, the vacation deserved by all, where no reservation is needed? Go Team You!

"I'm sorry, it's Thursday and the person that you are trying to reach has been temporarily disconnected, please try again later." Are you burnt out? Are you physically, emotionally and/or mentally exhausted? Well, disconnect! If only for a few moments, steal away time for you to slow down, pull it together and smell the roses. You want to offer the world your best but you can't when you are running on fumes. Only you know what you need, may it be "Calgon take me away," or quiet time with a friend, a book or simply with yourself... do it. Refresh, recharge and rejuvenate that wonderful person you are, your world is waiting. **Go Team You!**

Make me beautiful, pleaseeee… I love working out (I do!), shopping, dressing-up, putting on make-up and trying to make myself presentable to the world. I don't believe I am alone in this effort…men and women alike spend a fortune on looking their best. I believe everyone should invest in how they look if it makes them feel good but let's not stop there. Time, effort, obedience, faith and self-love are needed to complete who we are. It is the beauty that lies within that takes us to the next level. A beauty that is neither vain nor shallow. One that encompasses all that the Lord bestowed on us and that we have cultivated. We can't let that beauty get tossed aside or ignored because that one is everlasting. Go Team You!

The tooth is under the pillow. Santa is coming down the chimney, the Bunny will drop off the baskets in the morning and losing your teeth can make you rich. We have believed in many things because people we trusted told us to believe and the evidence was there to back it up. So when did we stop believing in the person we see every day in the mirror? We don't go after who or what we want because we don't believe…We don't say what we want because we don't believe…We suffer because we don't believe… Did anyone you trust, tell you to believe in yourself? If not, I am telling you, today and if you forgot, this is your reminder. God created you because He doesn't just believe; He knows what you are capable of. Santa, Ms. T. Fairy, Mr. BUNNY and you…making the impossible possible! **Go Team You!**

"On the road, again! I can't wait to get on the road again..." Whoever wrote that song had very different interest than me! I usually detest sitting and being confined for any length of time but that contradicts my philosophy that everything happens for a reason and we should get something from every experience. As I prepared myself mentally for my seven hour trek from SC to MD (I did it in six but that's another story), I analyzed my environment and tried to understand what if anything I could get out of this experience. I had three of my children held captive with no real distractions so within ten minutes we were talking about sensitive issues that they needed to discuss and that I needed to muster up the courage to address. Don't let any moment go by without understanding the opportunity component. Now, I can't wait to get on the road, again! Go Team You!

Don't allow your life to become like a gym membership. You join, pay your dues, buy the spandex, take two classes, do a set on the weights, do a run that looks very similar to your walk and then never participate again!! Get up, get exhilarated! Throw caution to the wind AND WORK IT OUT every opportunity you get!! Get your life into shape! Go Team You!

Registering a new day in my physical body, I open my eyes to the light. Realizing a new opportunity in my spirit, I open my eyes to the Light of the World. Slowly I stretch preparing my physical body for the day of wear and tear that lay ahead. Ever so cautiously, I stretch my spirit around my blessings, grateful for the day before me and anxiously awaiting all that He will entrust me with today. I rise, spirit and body, "Good" Morning. Go Team You!

Today I eavesdropped, not intentionally but accidentally (is that possible?). A foreign gentleman who was excited about his first trip to the US started talking excitedly about all that he had seen and experienced since landing here, to a woman that sat next to him on the metro. He brought out the camera, shared his photos and explained to her where his adventures had taken him. What a beautiful sight to watch her listen, smile, nod and respond to her new companion. So often, we are caught up in our own world and disconnected from the world around us that we forget about the art of listening, sharing and being a part of our present environment. Let's connect again; someone has something to say to us. Go Team You!

Marco!!! Polo!!! Marcooooooo!!!!! Polo!! There is nothing like chasing after life blindly and never feeling as though you can catch up with it. You feel life calling you from all directions but which way to go? Marco!! You turn to the right just to find out that you are headed nowhere. Polo!!! Trying to answer life's calls on your own in the dark may leave you frustrated. Open up your eyes to the Light and follow His voice calling your name!
Go Team You!

"Stuck," can that be a positive thing? I suppose you can put a positive spin on anything but it may take some effort. I do believe when my British flying companion used the word "stuck" when describing living in SC, there weren't many warm and fuzzy feelings floating around in his head. We must be careful with what words we choose when describing our current state of affairs. Sometimes it is very easy for our words to dictate our feelings. Now I, on the other hand, was really "stuck" as I sat in window seat 36 in front of the bathrooms and next to 18 month old Oliver who screamed 2/3 of our 15 hour flight but I would like to prefer to refer to my situation as "happily contained!" Go Team You!

If you missed something you can always Rewind, if you are interrupted, please push pause until you can resume where you left off. If you want to plan for the future, fast forward to where you would like to be eventually just don't forget to press play and enjoy the current moment. Rewind and let's review where we came from. Pause; take note of what worked and how to improve upon what didn't work as well. Fast forward and develop what your dreams and goals should look like now simply play. Go Team You!

it all that you hoped it would be? Do you feel Relief? What about Satisfaction, do you feel a little of that? The planning for this excursion took effort! Takeoff was bumpier than you had anticipated and the flight may have had significant turbulence but you didn't abandon the mission nor did you turn around midstream. You stayed course and now you have landed...did you remember to thank your copilot? Go Team You!

Today is a "don't stand in your own way" day! Go Team You!

Little Miss Muffet sat on her tuffet eating her curds and whey. Little Miss Muffet when will you get off your tuffet? When things go my way. Oh dear, oh dear but that time may not be near and you are wasting your life away. Stop eating, stop pouting, stop waiting for change today is here, you're wasting it, that's clear it's time to go out and play! Go Team You!

In life indecision sometimes equates to those times we don't want to decide even though we know what is right; immaturity is when we choose that maturity is not fun; imbalance is when being out of whack is easier than keeping all of the balls up in the air and insanity is our plea when holding it together seems impossible. So how do we make the mature decisions and balance our sanity? PRAYER! Go Team You!

Hooray!! It's Unpacking Day! Unpack the hurt that you said you had walked away from but seems to be taking up valuable space in your life bag of hopes, dreams and aspirations. As we dig deep in the bag and unpack the stinky, dirty laundry that has taken up much needed space in are already overweight luggage, we begin to make room for the necessities that will help us survive the adventure that lays in front of us! Go Team You!

Just because you got a bite on your hook doesn't mean you've caught dinner!

I just heard the news!!!! What a blessing!! What will you do with such an outstanding prize?!?! Don't squander it!! Be grateful because some that win simply don't appreciate how awesome it really is!! Again, CONGRATULATIONS on winning...ANOTHER DAY!!! Go Team You!

If we invest 0% of our God given gifts and talents into achieving our dreams, why are we waiting on Him to give us a return on our investment?! Go Team You!

Worry: unwanted thoughts of discouragement, dismay and disappointments.
Do: Delete before damage disables you.
Don't: Declare defeat to the devil.
Go Team You!

Wake up from your deep slumber. You have rested long enough. Open your eyes to a new day filled with new promises, opportunities and hopes of a better you. Get up and stretch, breathe and prepare. Wash off the remnants of yesterday and dress yourself for a brand new beautiful present! Go Team You!

"Awesome" according to Webster's means: "extremely good."
YOU ARE AWESOME...so now what are you going to do? Go
Team You!

Good morning, sunshine! Good morning, rain! Good morning, hurt! Good morning, pain! No matter what is waiting, this morning is "good" simply because it came. Go Team You!

"SLIPPERY WHEN WET - NO running, NO skipping, NO jumping - SLOW DOWN, Watch your step, Proceed with CAUTION" - Read the signs, WHEN CONDITIONS BECOME HAZARDOUS TO YOUR HEALTH! Go Team You!

Remember this race has already been won; we just have to cross the finish line! Go Team You!

Good morning!!! Would you like to Super Size your order today? Wonderful! So I have 2 orders of blessings, an order of expectations and 3 side orders of healing; all Super Sized. Your payment is... your FAITH! Go Team You!

We roll the life dice but we choose to skip our turn waiting for a better roll therefore, we fail to move ahead to the next space. It is now Johnny's roll and he moves ahead again and again. We watch him as he plays the game of Life, laughing, excelling and receiving the treasure chest cards, which seem to offer him all the prizes that we want!! "How come Johnny keeps winning," we whine. Did he learn a trick to rolling the dice or is he just lucky? No, Johnny learned early on in the game, that regardless what you roll you must continue to play the game otherwise you lose! Go Team You!

I will do what I must to develop trust. No, it doesn't even matter that others' actions are unjust. I will forgive them as they are, even though they try to leave a scar. Why, you ask. Because my Father is my guiding star and my lot in life is to follow Him no matter how far. Go Team You!

Is your shoe untied? Is the sun blinding? Are you afraid of stepping in puppy presents? No? Then stop moving here and fro with your eyes hung low! I caught you!! There is an entire world in front of you. So lift your chin, throw back your shoulders and enjoy the view! Someone just walked by trying to catch your eye and just say "hi!" Go Team you!

Who were you yesterday? Do you feel dismay about who is looking back at you in the mirror today? Did you pray and say, "Lord, mold me, for I am your clay?" Or did you relay to others their power to dictate, determine and decide the "you" that would come out to play? Don't you dare give that power away! Go Team You!

"...birds fly over the rainbow, why oh then why can't I?" You can!! Leave your nest of comfort-ability. Extend your wings of dreams and expectations. Soar over limitations, nay sayers and the impossible. Fly to new heights and don't look back! You are free to believe it, to receive it and to achieve it. So go get it! Go Team You!

I hate going to the Doctor. Yes, he/she may be the expert but I want to diagnose, prescribe and nurse myself back to health rather than to seek the help of a professional. There are times in our lives when we cannot heal ourselves. We must realize our limitations and seek help from a Higher Power. The road to recovery can be a smoother and faster one if we are NOT DOING THE DRIVING! Go Team You!

Perfect we are not. Our mistakes, hopefully we do not plot. Of course, we must pay, when we sometimes go astray but He does forgive, so it will be okay. We must simply drop to our knees and pray. Go Team You!

If you don't take your foot off the brake, moving forward is not possible. So today, adjust your seat, set your radio to your favorite station, check your mirrors, slowly release the brake and move on with your life! ROAD TRIP! LITERALLY. Go Team You!

"Step on a crack break your mama's back, step on the line break your daddy's spine!" When I was little, I used to trip all over myself trying to avoid cracks, lines, ladders, broken mirrors and spilt salt but the reality is, "bad things" happen. We can't avoid, circumvent or hide from them. What we can do is learn from them, rise above them and minimize the impact of them on our lives. Most importantly we must remember to praise Him as we go through them because He can heal our mama's back, our daddy's spine, restore the broken mirror, remove the ladder and count the grains of salt as he cleans up our "oops" for He is God! Go Team You!

"Please, PICK IT UP!" Apparently, my children's eyesight is failing because I am the only one that can see "stuff" on the floor!! They walk over "stuff" without blinking an eye!!!! How often do we walk over "stuff?" Have we gotten to a point that we, too, don't see "stuff," or DO WE SEE IT AND SIMPLY IGNORE IT? Let's PICK our "stuff" UP and deal with it before we trip and hurt ourselves!!! Go Team You!

He loves me. He loves me not. He loves me. He loves me not. He loves me (unconditionally!!!!)...are you smiling, now? Go Team You!

Okay, how will we do this? Hmmm. Is there anywhere to place your foot? Keep looking, please. Really? Nowhere? Let me see if I can find a rope... Nope. No rope. So here is my final suggestion: drop to your knees and ask the Lord to destroy the wall that you have built around yourself. Once He removes it, please stop constructing. Walls made of hurt, fear, un-forgiveness and anger, go up quickly, and are virtually indestructible. Don't continue to live behind that wall, ask Him for a hand. Go Team You!

Are you out of gas? Stalled? Has your battery simply died? Call AAA (the Able & Awesome Almighty) because He can give you jump or tow wherever you NEED to go. Go Team You!

It is time for silence. Shhhh. Not a time to talk but a moment to be muted. Shhhh. Turn off the thoughts, responses and opinions that want to escape and be heard. Shhhh. Offer a quiet nod, a touch of support or simply a smile. Shhhh. Let your silence speak for you. Just Listen...Shhhh...Someone needs you... Go Team You!

You Have been chosen to participate in the ultimate game of "follow the Leader" aka "Head of the line!!" Are you ready? Of course, you are because He has specifically chosen you to be on His team and to follow Him!!! The rules are simple to understand but extremely difficult to follow but not impossible. The leader has already been chose, so our task is to mimic His actions. If for any reason we decide to fall out of line or to stop mimicking Him, we are out. WAIT! WAIT! Don't panic! THE GAME IS NOT OVER! I REPEAT, THE GAME IS NOT OVER!! If we go to Him and ask for another opportunity to follow Him, He will let us play again! Sooooooo, on your mark, get set...FOLLOW!! Go Team You!

Did you do it?!?? Did you??! You are quiet...I did and I feel wonderful! Yes, I know things are not perfect and yes, I am still hurting over that thing and no, I didn't get an opportunity to work on those items and...none of that matters!!! I THANKED HIM ANYWAY - in the middle of it ALL!!! Go Team You!

"So long, farewell,au Wiedersehen, goodbye"
Now slowly turn. Open the door and go through it. Shut the door
behind you, put the key in, lock it, walk away and DON'T
LOOK BACK! DON'T!! JUST KEEP WALKING!
The time has come to say goodbye. It is difficult, we know! We
have all been there. It is important that you don't turn back, you
can't return back there again! You can do this! We believe in
you! Move on! Proceed forward! That door is now closed! Go
Team You!

I wake each morning searching for my glasses so that I can bring clarity to a new day. Most mornings I can't find them so I forge ahead without them. I rely on my "Morning Eyes" to see letters and make words. We are ever so reliant on everything (and/or everybody) around us to help us see our lives that we forget, at times, our own strengths and capabilities. Isn't it time for all of us to rely on our own "Morning Eyes," to bring clarity to our lives? (This message was written with my morning eyes so I hope everything is spelled correctly otherwise my theory is out the window!!) Go Team You!

"Slippery when wet!" CONDITIONS HAVE CHANGED IN A BLINK.OF AN.EYE - CAUTION IS NEEDED!!! Please adjust, adapt and rethink your movements before proceeding forward. If you don't implement immediate adjustments when needed, problems may occur. Forward movement is always, possible just be constantly aware of your environment and changing conditions. Go Team You!

Oh Geesh, I am up three! It's so dark I can't even see, so on the way to the bathroom I bumped my knee! Ouch! Now I am lying in bed not able to sleep, wishing I had the key to stop worrying about things that bother me. I decide the answer is to say a plea to my Father. So I close my eyes and listen for Thee, and soon He whispers, "your worries and problems you cannot flee but you can find rest if you simply trust in Me." Go Team You!

Food for thought: Everyday without fail we brush our teeth (at least I hope we do!). Why? To remove all the yuck that has built up within us and after brushing we feel refreshed and renewed. Now how is that different from prayer? Pray daily...Go Team You!

WIPEOUT! My children love the show Wipeout! It is a program where contestants try to complete an outrageously wet and unpredictable obstacle course. They are punched, prodded and foreign items are thrown at them, while they jump, climb and pray their way to the finish line. As an observer, I often ask myself is it really worth the prize to subject yourself to what they go through? But in the end, you really must admire the victor; the one who would not be defeated and who was determined regardless of the odds, to finish the course that he started. Go Team You!

Picture this: Madison Square Garden is packed! The crowd is going wild! Bets are being placed, announcers are spewing off at the mouth their opinions and the time for action is drawing near!!! But wait! Where is our shining star of the night? You are in a holding room anxious, excited and sweating bullets! The time has come for you to fight the good fight. In the ring, your opponent, Life, is waiting to pummel you. Will you put on your boxing gloves and take life on or will you hide out in the holding room and hope Life gets tired of waiting and leaves? The crowd is cheering you on, God is in your corner, Go out there and be the Victor! **Go Team You!**

SAVOR THAT… an Angus New York Strip Steak seasoned and cooked to perfection… SAVOR THAT… the perfect kiss on the beach when the sun is setting… SAVOR THAT… the "perfect moments"…SAVOR THEM. Here comes the problem: once the steak is finished you may feel sluggish…weeks after the kiss on the beach, the relationship may be over and the "perfect moments" may have evolved into not so happy tomorrows BUT the aftermath should never diminish the moment that you put the first succulent piece of steak in your mouth, or the excitement that engulfed you during the kiss. Savor those moments and hold on to how they made you feel as you were going through them don't get stuck on what happened next. Go Team You!

My Aunt was Jackie Robinson's Godmother, so as a child I spent time at his home in Connecticut playing. Annually his foundation sponsored a jazz concert which took place on his estate and I met some of the greatest jazz artist of our time. All of this greatness surrounded me and I was too young and naive to appreciate the life I was living. How Humbling. This morning as I lay awake and I thanked my Heavenly Father for my undeserved Blessings it dawned on me that again I am too young and naive to appreciate the life I am living. I have a PERSONAL RELATIONSHIP WITH THE ALMIGHTY! There is no one higher and yet He knows my name and loves me unconditionally!! Oh how wonderfully humbling. Go Team You!

…when the bough breaks, the cradle will fall, and down will come baby, cradle and all. Sometimes it is not what you say but HOW you say it. Everyone is familiar with Rock a Bye Baby. It is a lullaby, with a tragic ending, that we sing to SOOTHE our precious little ones. Every day we are given multiple opportunities to interact/communicate with others. It is up to us on HOW we communicate our message. Our delivery can make people receptive to what we are saying like a baby to a lullaby OR we can turn our listener against us like the crazy nanny in the movie "the Hand That Rocks The Cradle." You decide. Go Team You!

Just lyrics to a song or words to live by? You decide…Shake it up baby, twist and shout!! It is TIME! Come on, come on, come on baby now: Don't wait another minute! The moment is now to SHAKE UP YOUR LIFE. TWIST the top off of your ever day routine. SHOUT AT THE TOP OF YOUR LUNGS… "I am blessed" and no day has to be the same as the day before. It is all up to you! Today is a new day! Come on and work it on out! Go Team You!

Last week I hurt my foot and I had a, not so cute, limp. As a result, I was suffering from high heel withdrawal and I resembled a lost puppy! At first glance, people commented that the pep in my step was gone and then they mentioned my shrunken stature (NO HEELS). Finally, they all tilted their heads to show me concern and pity, what an uncomfortable state to be in…needy, unstable and somewhat vulnerable. As I walked to a presentation with a colleague, who is like a mother to me, I put my arm in her's and she instantly transformed into my "human crutch." She slowed to my pace, supported my limp and soothed me with her calming manner. What a beautiful moment. We all need that every once and awhile. Can you be someone's "Human Crutch?" Someone you know may be injured or hurting, why not be what they need to move forward. Go Team You!

Do you have yucky stored up in a bottle? You know those feelings that gnaw away at you regarding something that felt significant when it occurred but over time, you have forgotten the ingredients that were used in creating the yucky but the feelings are still there. Let's discuss briefly the drawbacks to this bottle of yuck, shall we? Eventually the "yuck" oozes out because the bottle can't contain it. It gets all over everything around it, like a broken ink pen in an oversized purse. Don't allow stale feelings to impact your opportunity to enjoy fresh hopes. So take the top off the "yuck" slowly and pour it down the drain. Rinse out the bottle with God's promises and refill it with a 1/4 cup of optimism, 1/2 cup of faith and top it off with laughter! Go Team You!

"MEMBERSHIP HAS ITS PRIVILIGES!" To sign up for a credit card you have to meet a number of criteria such as, a specific income level, good credit which demonstrates your ability to repay your debt in a timely fashion and complete an application that must be reviewed. I have great news about a membership that the perks are out of this world, your past is forgiven, the ability to pay back the credit that is extended to you is not considered and all you have to do is say "yes, Jesus You are my Lord and Savior." Go Team You!

the covers, no one can see me. As a child, I truly believed that was true (don't pretend you didn't do the same!). As adults, we sometimes try to relive this exercise. If we remain perfectly still, head under the covers, no one will see or bother us. Really? Well, eventually I figured out that I could still be seen when my head was under the cover. Besides being hot and feeling as though I was going to suffocate, nothing came from me hiding myself. Live life outside of the covers!! Everyone can see you and there is no living if you're hiding! Go Team You!

80/20, 60/40, 50/50 - How much are you willing to give up? A good friend recently explained to me the 80/20 rule. Basically, it boils down to: you can't always get 100% so will you be okay with 80? This concept may come to play when choosing your partner, raising your children or even when pursuing your goals. I personally never want to settle yet there does come a time when we must realize that what we have imagined in our mind's eye may not take on the same form in our reality and that's okay. Less than 100% doesn't equate to failing. Sometimes it is important to get a, 20/20 perspective on our lives and come to an understanding with ourselves that happiness can be achieved at different levels. Go Team You!

And then I smile? After a glorious weekend and a few days off, I returned to a mess at work. I Had a rush project, broke my glasses, spilt cranberry juice all over my documents, did not get to eat lunch until 3, ripped the back of one of my favorite dresses and for an encore I broke my shoe on the way to the metro (yes, they were so old that Wilma Flintsone probably had a pair but still!!). And still I smile? It was one of those days where you throw up your hands and wait for lightening to strike! And still I smile? Then you are confronted with the images of the bombing victims in Boston or the sadness in Syria and the hungry in Africa…AND STILL I SMILE!!! Go Team You!

Hide and go seek is a simple game. Your heart beats out of control as you try to seek out the perfect hiding place. Once you have found it, you do all you can to stifle your giggles so you don't give your secret location away and then you wait quietly. The adult version of this game is similar minus the giggles. Instead of hiding in a closet, we hide behind imaginary walls. These walls can take the form of our work, responsibilities or simply our fears. We don't let anyone know about our secret location and we quietly proceed with our life, waiting. Only problem is no one is seeking us out and calling us from our hiding place. Come out! Come out! Run to home base and join the game of life. Go Team You!

Good day! Have you been waiting long? Please follow me to our smaller waiting room and someone will come and get you shortly. (time passes....lots of time) Well hello. Please follow me to the examining room. Thank you for your patience, you will be seen shortly. -- SOMEONE IS WAITING ON YOU! As you go from one aspect of your life to another, knocking on doors and entering into situations that are not meant for you, He continues to wait. Is it fair, moving Him from one waiting room in your life to another until you are ready to examine Him in all His glory!? Fortunate for us He is "patience" and He's not going anywhere, but we may want to knock on his door next and focus on what He needs from us! Go Team You!

IT DOESN'T FIT!!! Round hole…square block. As toddlers we bang it, throw it, try again and eventually we realize that the square block doesn't fit the round hole. So we try the other slots until we figure out where it does fit. As we mature we begin to regress slowly (or in my personal case, somewhat rapidly). We constantly want to JAM the square block into the round hole. We KNOW it doesn't fit! Everyone around us told us it doesn't fit! Jesus, Himself, let you know it doesn't fit and yet and still you break out the sand paper because you are GOING to make it FIT!!! Well, NO MORE!!! Either put down the block and walk away from it or ask God to simply guide you so that you can place that block in its proper slot! Go Team You!

The chapter no one ever tells you about! Sometimes it hurts. Sometimes there are tears. Sometimes there is frustration. Man, woman, young or old, it doesn't matter, no one is immune to life's dark pages. It feels like a lonely place but not a place where you are alone. When the pen falls from our hands and the story plot takes an unexpected twist, what do we do? Do we give into the darkness and fight against what lurks around us or do we turn to the light of the MASTER EDITOR and request a rewrite? Go Team You!

What do Zoro, a raccoon, you and yes, even me, have in common? We all shop at Mask-r-us. At work/school we hide behind the mask of "phony smiles and agreeable nods" When dating or in social settings we wear the mask of "like me please." Even amongst some family members, we still can't go mas- less because we must wear the mask of "keep the peace." There is someone who sees beyond the mask and loves you for who you are unconditionally. With Him you can be yourself, relax and regenerate. So don't forget to take off the mask today even if it's for a brief moment - unmask. (On the other hand, some of us may need to borrow a mask or two!). Go Team You!

Peekaboo…I see you, but can you see yourself? I see you making that mistake. I see you hurting yourself. I'm watching you go the wrong way down a one way street and I can't stop you. Peekaboo, I will continue to see, watch and support you but sometimes as a friend or family member we must remind ourselves we can't control someone else's life. We also don't ever have to give up on them just because their volume is down and they can't hear us. Keep them in prayer and maybe one day their mute button may be off. Go Team You!

We at Happy Hunters United (HHU) Want You!!!! As the President and ONLY member of HHU, people often ask me about my consistent state of euphoria. Is my life any easier than others? Anyone that knows me or even spends five minutes with me would answer that with a resounding NO! So how do I live life with a smile on my face and a song in my heart? Because I CHOOSE to, each and every day that I rise. And guess what? You too, can be happy by simply joining Happy Hunters United!! The only prerequisite is that you recognize that you are BLESSED and that nothing that comes your way can change that fact. Go Team You!

The light is red and your seat belt feels as though a boa constrictor has attacked your entire body as you try to scratch an itch behind your left ear. Your eyes shift quickly from your rear-view to the traffic bearing down from your left. Then it happens, someone pulls up behind you and the pressure is on to make a right-hand turn on a red light! Sometimes all we need is a slight push to get out there and get going. Don't feel compelled to jump out into traffic if you are truly not ready (we wouldn't want you to get hit) but if the opportunity presents itself then don't worry about the oncoming traffic, tightening seat belt or anxiety swelling up in your throat- take off and make that turn on red! Go Team You!

UGH!! I did it! I didn't want to do it and I put it off for months! There comes a time when you have to face the un-face-able! We can't turn away from the uncomfortable and act as though reality will never catch up to us and say "tag your it!" Yes, yes, I know life is challenging enough without us seeking new challenges to conquer. But guess what? We can, are able and will conquer if we look into the face of what tries to defeat us and look up to the One that can help us. With all of that said, I AM STILL THROWING THAT BATHROOM SCALE OUT WHEN I GET HOME!! Go Team You!

Ouch! I know that hurt, I'm sorry. Oops! That was my fault, please forgive me. Oh no! My mistake, I apologize. Oh my, my, my-what a shame when hurt is caused and the words to heal are not spoken. Oh geesh - Why do we hold back the words "you hurt me," or "I'm sorry?" Oh Lord, please give us the strength to put aside our pride, fear or whatever holds us back from saying the words that can begin repairing damaged relationships. Go Team You and fix it today! Yay!

I'm not picking on you, I promise, but how many people do you speak to in a day? Now of those, how many do you actually stop to "listen" to their responses? Are you guilty of doing the "Howareya?" and run? We all can easily fall into that trap! At times, we simply get lost in our own thoughts and speak in passing to be courteous but not concerned. Sometimes, like robots, we may even say "good, good" to the person we ask before they have a chance to open their mouth! What if their response was, "horrible" and we missed it? Today, let's Stop, Ask, Listen and Respond. Someone may need only that from us to make a difference in their day. Go Team You! Yay!

Shoes, bags and dresses, Oh my!!! Sneakers, slacks and suits, Oh my! So we find our heroes lost in the outlet jungle, armed only with a credit card (that comes with a hefty 17% interest rate!). Attacked by clearance racks, tax-free weekend and additional 70% off discounts, they are weakened by the desire to buy, buy, buy, even though they need ABSOLUTELY nothing!!! What will they do? Where's the Wizard when you need him? There is a way out and it's not the clicking of the red shoes!! They simply must destroy the devious credit card that lured them into the jungle to begin with!! Once destroyed and all the bills that he created are defeated, our heroes can return to a stress-free walk in the park! Go Team You!

Extinction is near! Sitings are far and few between! Hope is waning but not all is lost! Experts have been consulted and the consensus is that HAPPINESS still does exist! According to the Matthew, Mark, Luke and John Survey Poll, complaining, self-pity and un-gratefulness are the top factors killing off our happiness. It has been confirmed that a simple "thank you" daily and recognition of the Father's role in our lives can bring, peace, confidence and yes, happiness...spread the word and help save happiness!! Go Team You!

There was an old woman who lived in a shoe…This old man came rolling home…Ole King Cole was a merry old soul…I've joined the club, I'm getting old!! I have reached the time of my life that I start use sayings like, "I remember when…" and "You young folk..." And guess what? I am happy about it! Many people fear aging and the images of living in a shoe, rolling home and even being a merry old soul, conjures up feelings of woe is me instead of what a blessing! "Know thyself," for me, signifies peace and contentment. This comes with time, experience and self-awareness. Pease is mine, happiness is mine and an everlasting internal smile is mine which all evolved as I aged. So today, I thank God for the opportunity to say "I'm getting old!" Go Team You!

I didn't know!!! Why didn't anyone tell me? I'm so sad and hurt! Now that I know, I will join the search!! When did you go missing?! When I saw your picture on the side of the milk carton, I was brought to tears. I lost myself once (okay maybe more than once, those teen years were a little sketchy!) but thanks be to God, I found my way home again and now when I look in the mirror, I feel good about the person looking back at me. Don't be ashamed to scream out for help when you're lost. God will head up the search party and lead you home. Go Team You!!

So imagine there was a site where people were rated and reviewed daily like hotels and restaurants!!! Would you receive an average star rating of 4 or 2? Would people refer you to their friends as "a person that others should know and spend time with," or "someone that should be avoided like the plague?" Now imagine how you would feel if Jesus scanned this site. Remember: you never know Who is watching!! Go Team You!

"On the road again I can't wait to get on the road again." Really?! Not so much! I detest sitting and being confined in a car which directly contradicts my philosophy "every experience is an opportunity." During my trek from SC to MD, I examined my opportunities -three of my children held captive!!! Within ten minutes, we were talking about sensitive issues that they needed to discuss and that I needed to put on my big girl pants and share with them. What a fabulous moment!! Don't let ANY experience escape without you reigning in the opportunity and making something valuable that enriches you! Go Team You!

Hello and welcome to the Cinderella Coping Club (CCC), where our motto is: No wicked step-mother can stand in our way, because we got this! Here at the CCC we focus on a balanced lifestyle. Yes, we believe in working hard but at the end of the day, you must be ready to put on the glass slippers for a night on the town. Our members are from all walks of life and they will support you even after the clock strikes 12. At CCC, we give you the tools to filter the verbal and emotional attacks from others, get the job done and still have a happy ending. No, we don't have a fairy Godmother at the helm (you got jokes?) but we do have our Father! Go Team You!

The top two uses for the tip of your tongue: 1. When trying to remember a word that is sitting on "the tip of your tongue," but refuses to come out, tap or tug on it slightly (this is a useful technique depending on your age - some of us can pull it out and still won't remember until about 3 in the morning when we should be sleeping!). 2. When you need to stop yourself from saying something derogatory, ugly or hurtful, BITE DOWN ON IT HARD!!!! Life is too precious, to be the originator of negativity. Go Team You!!

An external problem becomes an internal problem once you DECIDE to buy it for a price (that you can't afford!!). Once you own it and realize you can't fix, repair or salvage it, you may attempt to sell it, rent it or give it away and that is when you discover that no one else wants it!! Don't throw up your hands in despair because I know Someone who is willing to share the burden and see you through the rough spots if you Trust in Him. Do you know Him? If not, I would be happy to introduce you! Go Team You! Yay!

Rain, rain go away, come again another day: Little Arthur wants to play. Now Little Arthur, why must you wait for a sunny day? With a willing heart and your imagination (and a pair of galoshes, wouldn't hurt) you could make the most of any day! So, Little Arthur, please don't wait for perfect conditions to enjoy life because sunny days aren't always guaranteed. Go Team You!

For 18 long months, I lived half of my life in a car sitting in VA traffic. I sang, I chatted (not to myself, at least I can't remember doing that), I pondered life and I endured!! Since moving to MD my commute has become a breeze! Now, I don't just sing, I SING! I also admire the lush greenery (does Virginia even have trees) and I smile! This morning I thought about the horrendous journey that I had been on and how I hated every minute of it but without it how could I appreciate the journey I am on now.
Think about it... Go Team You!

Are you a flower that will flourish wherever it is planted? Or must you have the perfect conditions to bloom? Are your roots residing in fertile soil that keeps you strong? Are you being watered on a regular basis or receiving enough sun, which encourages growth? Have you stopped thriving, waiting to see what tomorrow brings? Today is here!!! Bloom where you are planted!! Choose to be strong and never stop growing regardless of your conditions. Go Team You!

As infants, our needs were met by being FED, CHANGED and COMFORTED. As adults, our basic needs haven't deviated but we tend to look in all the wrong places to FEED our souls, minds and bodies; to CHANGE our ideals, mindsets and outlook and to COMFORT our entire being. As babies, we HELD OUR ARMS UP and CRIED OUT to those you cared for us. As adults we must again CRY OUT and HOLD OUR ARMS UP but now it is to "HE" who ultimately cares for us. Go Team You!

Life is like gym membership... You join, because it is inevitable; pay your dues, because it is required; buy the Spandex (well not really sure why we buy the Spandex) and we participate initially because it is expected. Enough!! Today is the day we get EXHILARATED about this thing called LIFE!! Let's upgrade to PLATINUM MEMBERSHIP, WORK IT OUT AND GET OUR LIFE INTO SHAPE!! Go Team You!

...and on that farm he had a hen ee i ee i o. She spread her wings here and there and protected all who were near...oh, she was such a dear, ee i ee i o! And he had a mule that would not budge yet held a grudge ee i ee i o! There also was a cow that nourished and all around her folks did flourish; a dog that barked out of fear and; a duck that squawked when anyone was near ee i ee i o!!! Do you live here? Think about it...Go Team You!

You missed the signs!!! You lost direction. It's okay it could happen to anyone (and it does)! When we are not paying attention (and many times when we are...) it happens...WE RUN INTO A DEAD END! Sitting there baffled and mystified by the idea of not being able to go any further we waste life- minutes staring at a brick wall!! The impasse may have been placed there to protect us or to get us just to change our route. Whatever the reason (known or not)...TURN AROUND!! Go Team You!

A "FABULOUS" Day is one that happens on purpose. It is a day that you decide will unfold regardless of what people say, what things happen and how you feel. A "FABULOUS" day is easy to achieve when you understand that each breath that you breathe is not "a given" but "a gift " it's your choice what this day will look like and what this life will become....choose "FABULOUS" on purpose. Go Team You!

With eyes closed, weary from the game, we call out to life: MARCO!!! Career Life, responds: POLO!! So we chase after the incomplete projects, the unread reports and the tasks waiting our attention but we can't catch him! We call out, again: MARCO!! This time we hear Home Life responding loudly: POLO!! So we turn our attention and chase after the incomplete projects, the unopened bills and the tasks waiting our attention but again life alludes us and we can't catch-up. We call out once MORE tired, weary and frustrated: MARCO!!! God responds: HERE I AM...Game over! Go Team You!

What lurks in the shadows...UNDERNEATH YOUR BED?! I'm guessing something you shoved underneath there when you were cleaning and you promised yourself that you would deal with as soon as you had a chance. In the meantime, other items have compiled and items are now peeking out from underneath your resting place and you kick them back under as you pass by. In life, our problems are treated like the dusty stuff we have shoved into our dark spaces!! If we don't face them, it doesn't make them disappear. It's time to "clean house," and then we can rest comfortably. Go Team You!

When placed in a cool pot of water, an egg remains the same on the inside and out. When placed in a boiling pot of water, the same egg hardens on the inside and may crack on the outside. TODAY'S LESSION: Don't allow the situation that you find yourself in, transform who you are! Go Team You!

SKIP you!!! Don't fret, It simply means it wasn't your time to shine. Eventually you will get your opportunity to share with others what you hold in your "hand." Wait! Wait! Now, DRAW FOUR!!! Hey! It doesn't have to signify defeat. Sometimes we can't continue because we are forced to stock pile our arsenal to prepare for the battle ahead. REVERSE!! At times, you may have to go back in the direction you came but you are still in a position to win!!!! UNO!!!! keep striving for number 1, because you are a winner! Go team you!!

A TRUST Transformation:
T-Turn it over to the One who has equipped you for eternal life.
R-Remember where you have been and the battles you have won
and those that you have survived.
U-Unleash all that binds you to a life that doesn't bring you
peace and happiness.
S-Soak up your surroundings, the good, bad and the ugly - taking
what you need from each to grow
T-Trust...Simply Trust.
Go Team You!

A hush comes over the audience...hmmmm (Clearing throat). Tap, tap, tap...and a 1, and a 2, and a 1, 2, 3, 4. Your Symphony begins!! As the conductor of your life, you have to bring together many different sections with each playing a role in achieving a beautiful harmonious existence. Your spirituality must quietly play in the back-drop with no interruption while your family, work, dreams and self- preservation play against one another- ebbing and flowing. Remember, as you orchestrate your life, to keep the tempo and don't allow the music to fade. Go Team You!

The how to "Have a GOOD DAY ON PURPOSE" 3 Step guide:
1. Understand the magnitude of the "gift" that you were given by just being allowed to - WAKE UP!!
2. Then, simply say "Thank you."
3. Finally, engage the POWER/CONTROL that has been bestowed upon YOU, that allows YOU to dictate HOW YOU FEEL!! If YOU have decided to relinquish this control to someone else or something else (i.e. your spouse/partner or "wannabe" and/or your job!), please proceed immediately to the ONE who gave you the POWER initially, for support. If you have not given the power away or if you did, but recaptured it then YOU must CHOOSE to HAVE A GOOD DAY, on PURPOSE! Go Team You!

"We interrupt your regularly scheduled day to bring you this public service announcement: LIFE IS A BLESSING...ACT LIKE IT!!" "We now return you back to your life that's already in progress." Go Team You.

Registering a new day in my physical body, I open my eyes to the light. Realizing a new opportunity in my spiritual being, I open my eyes to the "Light of the World." Slowly, I stretch, preparing my physical body for the day of wear and tear that lays ahead. Ever so cautiously, I stretch my spirit around my blessings, grateful for yesterday and anxiously awaiting all that He will entrust me with today. We rise together, as one... the physical and the spiritual..."GOOD" morning! Go Team You!

Oh No!! I hope you didn't forget to make your reservation!! What reservation? Don't tell me... you did forget!! Yes, you made your flight and hotel reservations for your vacation. No, you didn't forget about the one at Booboo's favorite restaurant to celebrate that special occasion next week. With all that's on your plate, it may have slipped your mind, so I have to ask... did you remember to reserve your place in Heaven!? If you did not, no worries it's not too late! He is holding a place just for you. Just let Him know. And don't be shy, remind your friends to make their reservations, too. Once you do, you will double your reward points and THIS Life will never be the same! Go Team You!!

Uh Oh!! Did you drop a call AGAIN!?! Do you usually only have one or two bars or just lose the signal on a very annoying basis? Well I have just the service provider for you!! Get YAHWEH, THE ONLY "WAY" to stay CONNECTED!! With YAHWEH, communication is only interrupted if YOU decide not to use the service. No contract and no monthly fee or service charges!!! With YAHWEH you will ALWAYS be able to reach the ONE that matters!! So get YAHWEH TODAY and never be disconnected again!!! Go Team You!!!

The Washington Monument is recognized worldwide. Tourist come from the corners of the earth to see it, learn about it, take pictures of it, and most importantly appreciate it. Many of us that live near it have never been in it, don't know much about it and pretty much see it but don't really "see it." Often we lose sight of the Greatness that is right in front of us. We take ITS presence for granted and don't take the time to understand, learn and appreciate the AWESOMENESS that we have unlimited access to. Don't let another moment pass that you don't recognize the MASTER('s)PIECE that was created just for you. He's waiting...Go Team You!

Who is whispering in your ear and are you listening? When Dr. Martin Luther King Jr. was set to speak in front of the masses on August 28, 1963, he had a written speech ready to deliver. Observers of that day noted that he began to read from that speech, when Mahalia Jackson whispered to Dr. King "tell them about the DREAM!" The rest is HIStory. Who is whispering in your ear? Are you willing to change course mid-sentence to CHASE a DREAM? Shhhh... do you hear that? It's you opportunity to change YOURstory! Don't stand in your way! Go Team You!

We can go ANYWHERE if we can simply follow directions...The Global Positioning System (GPS) has the ability to guide us to destinations unknown, save us when we are lost, point out obstacles that lay in front of us and identify places that we may want to go, that we may not have realized are in our reach. Many of us put total confidence in our GPS and if we get lost, we usually take the blame for not understanding the GPS' instructions so we regroup and focus harder on what it is telling us to do. Do we rely on God's Perfect Son (the ultimate GPS) like that? Shouldn't we? Go Team You!

Surf's up!!! Wow!! Look at you riding that wave!!! Aaaaargh WIPE OUT! Okay, breathe deeply. Drowning is not an option. Panicking is not an option. Fighting against the waves drains your energies and leaves you limp and defenseless therefore, this, too, is not an option. Calm down. Yes, there you go. You are wearing a life-jacket therefore, you will be okay. You may take in a little water but you will survive and be ready to ride the wave again tomorrow! Go Team You!

This too shall pass..." The light will shine, again. The storm will subside. The wound will heal. In the meantime, WHILE in the dark, THROUGH the storm, and EXPERIENCING the pain, WE MUST: Keep our eyes open, Keep pressing through, Keep nursing the wound AND Keep the Faith. GO TEAM YOU!

The INEVITABLE, at times, is INDESCRIBABLE and almost IMPOSSIBLE to endure. That's when we must interject, I am blessed, I am grateful, I am a child of the GREAT I Am, and so I WILL be okay! Go Team You

Beyond understanding but for a reason- Nothing is by accident so look for your opportunity to grow and learn. It is among the wreckage. Go Team You!

OWWWWW! They simply don't fit!! OUCH! Yes, I totally agree they are very nice but if they don't fit... OOOO! STOP THE SUFFERING!! If they are causing pain, we must get rid of those, SHOES!! Why do we try to hold on to something that doesn't fit, causes us pain and may even rub us wrong and leave us disfigured and wounded?? TODAY WE MUST GIVE them away, RETURN them or just THROW them out (shoes, situations and/or person(s))!! There are some out there that are a better fit FOR US! Go Team You!

Diagnosis: WPA aka Wrong Person Allergy
Symptom: FREQUENT IRRITATION
Remedy: RUN (being alone is different than being lonely! - TRY
IT!)
GO TEAM YOU!

What have you done for me lately? When we are hungry, we work diligently to feed our Own appetite. When we are tired, we eventually lay OURSELVES down to sleep. Taking care of OURSELVES comes naturally; it is how we survive in the physical. It's time to now focus on our spiritual survival. Shifting the focus to THEM (whoever "them" may be). THEY are hungry and need to be fed. THEY are tired and weary seeking a place of rest. We were created to serve, to care for and to love. Whenever possible, be the food THEY NEED and A PLACE OF rest when THEY CANNOT GO FURTHER! Go Team You!

"Welcome back! Today we are talking to Rudolph about how he was bullied until Santa came along and pointed out his value." "Mr. Rednose, tell us how that made you feel." "Regardless, of how others viewed me, I understood my value and my worth. It was nice when Mr. Claus recognized my contribution to the team but my validation comes from the Lord." Go Team You!

HAPPY NATIONAL SHEDDING DAY!! Today we shed the old skin that is covered with past hurts, scars of disappointment, open wounds from those we didn't forgive and stains from tears of rage that we provoked. Beneath the old, you will find new hope, flawless forgiveness and unblemished dreams! Go Team You!

Today's assignment: Let's talk to people and not about them. Go Team You!

All RISE!! This is the case of Jack Sprat, who could eat no fat, vs. his wife, who could eat no lean, and so betwixt the two of them they licked the platter clean. Judge JC presiding! Jack: she won't! I tried! Mrs. Spratt: he doesn't! I can't! Judge JC: I HAVE! I CAN AND I WILL!! Sidebar: Has your Once upon a time lost its Happily Ever After? Take it to the JUDGE! Go Team You!

Hooray! Today is your "Make it Come True Day!!" It is time for what you THOUGHT was an impossibility in your mind to start becoming a POSSIBILITY in your reality. Release IT! BELIEVE IT! Achieve IT! Go Team You!

BREAKING NEWS: "The Devil finds work for idle hands to do." He is hiring the "bored," and the "woe is MEers" to work part or full time in the areas of sin, gossip and management. But DON'T PANIC, because GOOD NEWS has arrived!! The Father is recruiting!!! So let's be about our Father's business!! Go Team You!!!

"There's a hole in the bucket, dear Liza. Then fix it dear Henry."
Don't allow everything that is being poured into you to seep out!
Fix the holes so that you can OBTAIN, RETAIN and GAIN all
you need in order to be filled up! Go Team You!

You are wanted for the KIDNAPPING of your DREAMS, ASPIRATIONS, MOTIVATION and FAITH in your ABILITIES, TALENTS and GIFTS. God has paid the ransom, so we implore you to release yourself and live a life worthy of the price He paid! Go Team You!!

"You reap what you sow" SO, SOW SOMETHING
SPECTACULAR!! Go Team You!!

Hold on! Pull up! Hold on! Pull up! You got this! Just one more "Mental Chin-up" and success is yours!! Yes, I see the tension in your shoulders, the sweaty hands and the involuntary shaking! Your problems are weighing you down like bricks in your pockets but you are inches away from getting your chin over the bar! Don't give up now! We won't allow all the tension, sweaty palms and shaking deter us from pulling up to our goal and experiencing the glow of success! Go Team You!

In LIFE: INDECISION can run amuck when deciding means living with results we don't like. IMMATURITY will win out over maturity when it appears to make us happier (even if it is just for the moment); IMBALANCE may become our permanent address when the journey to balance seems too long and tiresome AND; INSANITY is simply our plea when holding it together seems impossible!! So in life, how do we make the MATURE DECISIONS and BALANCE our SANITY?? PRAYER! Go Team You!

Have you ever lost an Angel? "They are in a better place," they say. "I know," I say. I'm hurting because they are gone, I'm empty. Is it temporary sadness? No. Will it ease with time? Yes. God, please tell them I miss them and please hold my hand because I'm hurting…they're gone. Go Team You!

Why? Because, why? JUST BECAUSE! We have to have "just because," moments in life...just because. Those are the moments that may not be thought out, could be spontaneous and may have unexpected consequences BUT they make you feel good, put a smile on your face and fill you with laughter. Yes, we must be responsible when needed, we must lead when being followed and we must rise to the occasion when necessary but sometimes "just because," moments are our escape and give us momentum, just because! Go Team You!!

This is the day that the Lord has made...not simply the moment nor just the hour. It's not merely a figment of our imagination, a dream or a wish. Just as He created yesterday and as He will design tomorrow, He has given us a canvas to add color, energy and life!! Are we to complain about what we don't have, what we want and can't obtain? Do we cry about hurt, pain and or injury? Or do we, on "this day," REJOICE, be grateful for what we do have, what we've obtained and were given, not because of us but because of Him? This is the day!! Go Team You!

Your accomplishments belong to you. Your happiness is not being leased, it's yours. Your actions (positive or negative) are privately owned by you. Your words, thoughts, dreams and desires are all yours. Take responsibility for them...the good, bad and the ugly. To grow and manifest into a better you is to face who you are, your impact on others and admitting your role in the outcome of your life's situations. A better you resides in the (wo)man in the mirror...own it! Go Team You!!

Lend me your ear, please. I have a story to tell. It's a story of intrigue, tragedy, good times and bad. It's my story and although I am the author, it's my Editor that finished writing each chapter. When I thought all hope was gone, He allowed me to turn the page. What's your story? Are you struggling trying to write yourself out of your current situation? Put your pencil down...He will finish it for you. Go Team You!

It's time!!! Are you READY? Let's get STARTED with another version of the childhood favorite "Hide and SEEK!" As an adult, the game takes on a new twist...it's played alone!! That's right, no other players are necessary! Many of us are currently in the middle of a game where we are HIDING either from a situation or from facing ourselves regarding a situation that we should not be in. Or we are SEEKING someone or something that eludes us or, in all honesty, we are probably looking in all the wrong places. There is a version where every time you play, you win!!! The trick is to only HIDE in Him who will protect and watch over you...ALWAYS. AND to SEEK Him to fulfill ALL YOUR NEEDS! Go Team You!

Feelings are contagious. Sadness, disappointment, anger, resentment and frustration are easily spread like the common cold, infecting all those who come encounter with the inflicted. Let's preempt an epidemic by medicating early with a few doses of GMPM (God's Most Powerful Medicine)...His WORD!! Go Team You!

The poinsettia or as it is beautifully referred to in Mexico, "Noche Buena" (Christmas Eve) symbolizes what true giving means. Legend has it that a poor Mexican girl had no gift on Christmas Eve to take to church for the traditional Baby Jesus offering. She was terribly upset when she heard a voice say "...any gift you give out of love is worthy of the Baby Jesus." So she pulled some weeds along the way and once she placed them next to His crib, bright red flowers bloomed. It's not what you give in life, the beauty of your sharing only blossoms if your sharing is rooted in love. Go Team You!

RING, RING, RING!! RING, RING, RING!! He's calling, again. Why won't you answer? Yes, I know you know what he wants. Yes, I know he is relentless. But you can't continue to ignore him, that is simply impolite. I know your mother didn't raise you like that, so answer his call!!!! Stop walking away from him! He needs you to answer!! I'll answer for you!!! "Hello?" "Yes, please hold on." It's for you...it's Jesus. Go Team You!

Is it wrong to hope and believe in someone else? NO! Will they let you down? SOMETIMES! Will it hurt? PROBABLY! Do you stop hoping and believing in others? NEVER!! Go Team You! Are you ready for your REVOLUTION!!?! Go Team You!

Rise up and fight for a better YOU! Don't let the enemy get away with bringing you down just because the enemy looks familiar when you are standing in the mirror!! It's time for the motivated and positive you to take the negative, depressing and fearful you as a POW! Don't end up MIA during YOUR REVOLUTIONARY WAR!! REVOLT AND FIGHT FOR YOUR LIFE!!! Go Team You!

Guess who I met on the road to "I Must Yet, Become A Better Me? The Nay Sayers, who cried, "We bet you'll regret this journey, due to the trouble you will face." "That maybe true," I sighed "but I shall do it at my own pace!" "Turn back, before it's too late, you already have plenty on your plate!" "I do, I know but this is a place I must go because in this life we all must grow!!" Go Team You!

Let go of your ideals of perfection that satisfy only you and strive for a Purposeful life. Purpose being service beyond your comfort zone. It is outreach beyond your reach. You may find your Purpose hiding behind the uncomfortable or disguised in the difficult. Understand its value and know that it is necessary in the completion of "YOU" which is the definition of your existence. Love the Life you lead. Go Team You!

Slow down? Speed limits are determined on numerous factors such as the design of the road, environmental conditions and historical traffic patterns. They are posted along our journey for our protection as well as the protection of those around us. Many times, we ignore the warnings and our speeds exceed the limit. We cannot always see what's around the next curve, what icy conditions may lay ahead or what historically happened at that fork-in-the-road, so be cautious and conscious, heed the signs and enjoy the ride. Go Team You!

Something to contemplate...what is truly a monumental occasion that deserves to be celebrated? If you are enduring chronic debilitating pain, a moment of relief is monumental. If you are starving because there is no food source, receiving a slice of bread could be monumental. If you have been lost, with no direction, no destination and no guidance, being "saved," is monumental. Not suffering in pain, having food to eat and living a life with direction and purpose are all monumental events, are you celebrating? Go Team You!

The Crocodile Hunter studied, admired and interacted with crocodiles. He understood their behaviors, what made them act and react and that at a whim his life could be their next meal. The potential danger exhilarated him, their power intoxicated him and the teetering on the brink of death did not deter him. We watched him in awe because he lived in a world foreign from the one we reside in...or did he? We often wrestle our own crocodiles, by choice. We could walk away, run to shore and be safe but many times, we remain in a danger zone on our own free will. Many times, we don't understand the power, the behavior or the ability of the crocodiles in our lives. We, too, get exhilarated and intoxicated by the beast that captures our attention and we, too, teeter on the brink of emotional and spiritual deaths. Let's cage our crocodiles and return to higher ground. Go Team You!

252

Repeat after me:
Me: JOY
You: JOY
Me: HAPPINESS
You: HAPPINESS
Me: Peace of Mind
You: Peace of Mind
A good friend taught me about living in the "present moment."
Which means letting go of the past and allowing the future to
evolve naturally. There is power in our words and thoughts. Our
own words and thoughts dictate how we experience each and
every one of our God given moments. Only you can speak JOY,
HAPPINESS AND A PEACE OF MIND into your "right
now"...so give those words life! Go Team You.

Darkness engulfs you. The bed comforts you and sleep overtakes you....then SUDDENLY A BRIGHT LIGHT AWAKENS YOU!!! Do you cover your head, fighting off the light that is beckoning you out of your night cocoon OR do you adjust your eyes, push back the covers and walk into the light? Go Team You!!

When a baby cries due to discomfort, IT'S TIME FOR A CHANGE. When you run over a nail and the tire goes flat, IT'S TIME FOR A CHANGE. After a two-hour super intense zumba class, IT'S TIME FOR A CHANGE. When the tears come, things are deflated or downright stinky in your life, recognize the signs and know...IT'S TIME FOR A CHANGE! Go Team You!

Good morning to you, good morning to you, you've received a new day, so now what shall you do? Shall you complain and whine about the cold and how you struggle to get up because you feel so old OR SHALL YOU SHOUT ABOUT THE BLESSINGS YOU RECEIVE SIMPLY BECAUSE YOU BELIEVE!!?! Go Team You!!

Life's Blessings Snapshots can't happen unless you participate in life and know how to recognize a blessing. Capture the small moments that make life worth living...a smile, gratitude, love. File them away and look back on them when you forget how blessed you really are. Go Team You!

Wanting more is not a chore, just go and knock on opportunity's door. When it opens, walking thru is all up to you. It is imperative to believe and go do whatever is calling on you! Remember that you must be fearless and courageous to start something new! Don't ponder and wonder for too long because things can and will go wrong. Just simply pray, take the leap and be strong!! Go Team You!

From the creative mind of Claudia (my baby): if you can't FLY...RUN. If you can't RUN...WALK. If you can't WALK...CRAWL. JUST KEEP MOVING FORWARD!! Go Team You!!

"Don't poke the bear." When in bear country an encounter maybe unavoidable. Therefore, it's imperative that we are prepared and equipped for every situation. KNOW YOUR BEAR: It's important that you are able to recognize what you are facing. STAY ON MARKED TRAILS: Don't wander off path. REMAIN CALM: The bear smells fear. DON'T RUN!!! FIGHT AGGRESSIVELY FOR YOUR LIFE. Faced any bears lately? I have...Go Team You!

Can you find the possibilities in the impossible?
Have you moved pass the woe is me, and the belief that this is
what it will always be?
Did you realize that this day is the only one if its kind and that it
is filled with opportunities, dreams and blessings customized
especially for you?
You can, you have and you did? Then He will! Go Team You!

You are the house that God built!
This is the hurt that lives in the house that God built.
This is the pain that caused the hurt that lives in the house that God built.
This is the "Lord's Prayer" which you can pray every day, that can make the pain that caused the hurt to go away from the house that God built. Go Team You!

Make the call and make the difference. Make the first move and make an impact. Make someone smile and make an impression. Make this a year of gratitude and servitude with a beautiful attitude and make it a life worth living. Go Team You!

Can people CHANGE? YES! Can you CHANGE THEM? NO?
Can you CHANGE YOU? YES! Then what are we waiting for?
Frustration is born from trying to control what is not ours to
control. Go Team You!

No. No, really, I can't. Well, maybe. I shouldn't. Uhmmm.
O...okay? The ART of Persuasion. TV commercials, peers,
magazine covers at the checkout line and time-share sales people
selling you dreams, fun and quality time...regardless the form of
the persuasion, the objective is the same, to make you do
something that you had no intention of doing and IT WORKS!!
The Bible was created with the same objective. Pastors interpret
the parts we don't understand to persuade us to take heed and the
Holy Spirit lives in us, gnawing at our conscience to take a
different direction. Yet we appear, at times, to be immune to the
Lord's persuasion techniques. Why? After watching TV, we will
run out and buy the newest gadget, or when a friend wants to go
and we are exhausted we may still go, or pick up the newest
edition of a tell all tabloid to find out who is leaving who or buy
a piece of property that we own. for a week. Why? Go Team
You!

Is it wrong to hope and believe in someone else? NO! Will they let you down? SOMETIMES! Will it hurt? PROBABLY! Do you stop hoping and believing in others? NEVER!! Go Team You!

Hickory Dickory Dock, the mouse ran up the clock. Why? I don't know but he had a reason. Either it was something he wanted to do, was forbidden to do (and did it anyway) and/or was conditioned to do and did it out of habit. There is always a reason for our actions, if we want to admit to it or not. We are thinking beings driven by reasons. Therefore, let's be reasonable when deciding to run up the clock! Go Team You!

Lessons from a Cow's Digestive System (CDS). The CDS allows the cow to swallow their food whole (items that are indigestible, as well!). They then repeatedly regurgitate and re-chew the food or "cud" The cud is re-swallowed and further digested. What if we were to see God's Word as our ONLY food source (especially the indigestible parts -the bits we don't get). With the CDS approach we could swallow it whole. Then repeatedly regurgitate and re-chew on it until we are able to create CUD which would be to: CONSIDER what the Word means to us, UNDERSTAND how it fits into our world and DECIDE how we will use it. We would be fed, nourished and satisfied! Try the CDS approach today and never be hungry again! Go Team You!

The "Go Team You" Quality of Life Pledge:
I WILL CONTINUE TO "LIVE" EVEN WHEN "LIFE" GETS
IN MY WAY ! Go Team You!

Reruns! Reruns! RERUNS!!! Until you decide to turn the channel, you are stuck watching your life repeat one sad episode after another. Your service provider included a guide upon installation...check it out, review your options and then CHANGE THE CHANNEL. Go Team You!

We all know why the chicken crossed the road. What we don't focus on is what Charlie Chicken had to endure to get to the other side! Like what roadblocks did Charlie face? What types of aggressive, erratic drivers may have tried to run him down during his trek?! And was he truly equipped for bad road conditions!!?! We may never know the answers to any of these questions but one thing is for certain, Charlie had a goal...do you? And what will you endure to reach it? Go Team You!

You are all dressed up for the masquerade party and when you arrive, you find that you were misinformed and it's not a masquerade party BUT you can't get the mask off. Our life can resemble that scenario. At the job/school we are behind the "mask of work." When dating or in social settings we wear the "mask of like me, please." Even amongst some family members, we still can't go mask less because then we must wear the "mask of keep the peace." There is someone who sees pass the masks and loves you for who you are unconditionally. With Him you can be yourself, relax and regenerate. Don't forget to take off the masks today and free the real you.

All Rise!!! Do you swear to tell the truth the whole truth and nothing but the truth, so help you God? Oh, the stress! With sweaty palms and their collar tightening with each swallow the plaintiff tries to make his case. Shifting his weight from one foot to the other the defendant begins to twitch under the glare of the all powerful judge (yes, I watch too much Judge Judy!). Then the fate of the case is passed down! Oh, the intrigue! Are you ready for that day when you stand before the ultimate Judge? Our story, guilt and shame will already be revealed to the court and there will be no need to defend ourselves or plead not guilty. So what do we do? Let's start today to build our case by changing the evidence. Go Team You!

Sticks and stones may break your bones BUT NAMES CAN, DO and WILL cause permanent damage, especially sent by text! In this age of texting, we sometimes become too comfortable in substituting a text message for a phone call. I understand the convenience aspect but I also understand how text messages can be misinterpreted and lead to bad feelings, hurt egos and yes, even to the brink of break-ups! When a serious matter needs to be discussed or when a line of texting turns the wrong way down a one way street time to make a call. Old fashion? Maybe. Priceless? Most definitely! Go Team You!

What NOT to wear? Don't wear the cloak of invisibility! You were created to be seen, heard and your impact felt. When getting dressed daily remember to always dress for success, which goes beyond the clothing on your back. To be seen, hold your head high because you are a child of the Almighty. To be heard, speak words of positivity to those who seek your advice. To make an impact, hone your gifts and share them with the world. Go Team You!

Did you hear? Mother Nature is missing!! I knew something was wrong since I am freezing and June is right around the corner!! We come to expect some things to be the same in our lives always and forever. When we wake up to a Spring morning on the east coast of the US and put on sandals and a lovely Spring dress we don't expect for it to be 40 degrees! So when life's puzzle pieces don't fall into place we get out the "make it work" scissors to make them fit. Sometimes people don't behave the way we expect and things don't happen the way they have in the past. Do we throw up our hands and turn our back on life when it changes without our permission? NO!! We will adjust, adapt and put on an overcoat!

Challenge (yourself to dream). Conjur (up an idea). Consider (the possibilities). Create (ways to implement it). Capitalize (on your God given gifts -we all have some) Consult (with the Almighty). Carefully (listen for His response).Concentrate (on the positive). Complete (the dream). Change (the world). Go Team You!

Quiet, tip, tip, tip, tip, tip..."STOP TIP TOEING THRU LIFE!!!!! STEP INTO IT!!!!!!" Go Team You!!

Today is "National I Don't Wanna" Free Day!! To commemorate the holiday we are NOT allow to say any variation of the following: "I Don't Wanna try it, do it, taste it, hear it etc..." God has given us another day, let's "WANNA" live and experience it to the fullest! Enjoy your blessings!! Go Team You!

ENDLESS are the possibilities that are waiting for you today.
LIMITLESS is your potential when you believe in the "you" that
God created and not the "you" that you see in the mirror.
PRICELESS is the breath that you just took. How many of us
realized that?
WORTHLESS is a life that is not LIVED! Go Team You!

Awwww, what a lovely gift! I do hope you thanked the One who gave it to you...We have definitely gotten out of the practice of sitting down and writing thank you cards but I do believe a simple "thank you," will go along way, in this case. Many of us forget or take the gift for granted but I know you won't. Especially because you realize that breathing is a "gift" and not a "given." Go Team You!

We, again, interrupt your life to send you to the "GOTO" corner! In the "GOTO" corner (God Ordered Time-Out), "Some things," are prohibited (i.e. "something" to do, mad about "something," wanting "something," (that we usually don't need), going to buy/pickup/get "something," worried about "something")!!! In the GOTO corner, "some things" become nothings and there you can focus on the "RIGHT THING!" Go Team You!!

READY? Eyes shut! Head thrown back! Double over, gripping stomach, tears flowing and mouth wide open!! LAUGHTER, a beautiful sight!! It's addicting and contagious!! Try it for yourself...It heals, the hurt!! Go Team You!

Picture this, my family, which at any time can include anywhere from 5-50 people (we are a loving bunch), in beautiful Amsterdam! I, like Julie from the Love Boat, am always the entertainment Director, so I had decided that we were going to see the windmills! We rented the bikes, we were given the maps, the sun was shining and we were on our merry way! After 5 hours of riding, we concluded that we were lost and that we were not going to see any windmills that day (apparently map reading is easier in grammar school!). Do you know that was one of the best days of my life? I spent a glorious day with my family laughing and loving in the sun. Sometimes we have to remember that the destination may be a lot less important than the actual journey. Go Team You!

Remember when Jack, "fell down and broke his crown and Jill went tumbling after?" I am not sure who Jill was to Jack but I do know she cared enough to share in his suffering. Not too many of us will endure bodily harm for another but what would we do for another? Do you know someone who is in need of a friend, or someone just to listen to their woes? Why not be their Jill?

One day soon, you may be a Jack. Go Team You!

"Ladies and Gentlemen, we are beginning our descent and we'll be landing on the island of Excuse very shortly." "The Captain wanted me to remind you of a few housekeeping items before we land." "The island is covered with the "ICan't" bug. If bitten by one it will leave you incapacitated. We also suggested you don't visit the "Amen Corner." "Many badly afflicted residents of Excuse Island setup camp on this corner looking for new recruits." "Our final recommendation from the Captain is DON'T DISEMBARK THIS PLANE!!" "We are offering full refunds and vouchers to any passengers looking to try a different destination." "There are still flights available to Optimism and Hope, book your tickets TODAY!" Go Team You!

Welcome to the first day of try-outs for Go Team You! To qualify for the team you must be open to change, understand that you are not perfect, be willing to support your fellow team members, believe in yourself and more importantly, believe in Him!
Okay, we have watched you during the practices, we understand that you have Purpose and drive and we have decided that you are Go Team material! Welcome to the Team!

CPSIA information can be obtained at www.ICGtesting.com
Printed in the USA
LVOW01s2007090714

393589LV00023B/1151/P